DATE DUE

6/24/2008		

Demco, Inc. 38-293

RULES *for the*

Road

SURVIVING YOUR FIRST
JOB OUT OF SCHOOL

Eve Luppert

A Perigee Book

A Perigee Book
Published by The Berkley Publishing Group
A member of Penguin Putnam Inc.
200 Madison Avenue
New York, NY 10016

First edition: June 1998

Published simultaneously in Canada.

The Penguin Putnam Inc. World Wide Web site address is
http://www.penguinputnam.com

Library of Congress Cataloging-in-Publication Data

Luppert, Eve.
    Rules for the road : surviving your first job out of school / Eve Luppert.
       p.   cm.
    ISBN 0-399-52411-8
    1. Vocational guidance—United States.   2. Career development—United
States.   3. Youth—Employment—United States.   I. Title.
HF5382.5.U5L87   1998
651.14—dc21   97-35106
                                                                          CIP

Printed in the United States of America

10   9   8   7   6   5   4   3   2   1

To Steve Alburty, who made me write it

For my dad

CONTENTS

ACKNOWLEDGMENTS

MANY THANKS TO DOUG KNOPPER, WHO ACTUALLY UNDERSTANDS THAT FINANCE STUFF AND WROTE A first draft of the chapter on money for me. When he was done, even I understood it. Thanks also to Montana, who proofed the original manuscript, adding encouraging words and good advice as she went. I am also grateful to Faye Cone and Marian Salzman who helped me figure out what to do with the manuscript, Rene Cho who accepted and sold it and Michael Kenney who edited and helped me get it in order. Thanks to Chiat/Day and Jay Chiat who kept hiring me back when I'd run off to be an artist or something. I've been very lucky to have learned much of what follows from Susan Segall who gave me my first job, Sharon Stanley and especially Adelaide Horton, whose style and grace under pressure I will always aspire to and whose friendship I'll always cherish. Thank goodness for Susan Wands, her heart and her willingness to print this out a million times. Finally, I have the best brothers and sister ever and I adore them. Thanks Sylvia, Jiggs and Paul and all variations of Lupperts who give me everything that really matters.

Introduction

FINALLY! YOU'VE LANDED IT. IT TOOK PERFECT RESUME AFTER HUMILIATING INTERVIEW AFTER PAINFUL COVER letter. You've been sweating getting a job since your last semester in school; it's probably all you've thought about. OK, it's not all you've thought about. Getting this job may have taken you anywhere from two weeks to six months. You bought the helpful book about how to write a power resume, how to ace the interview, and how to write a charming yet informative cover letter. You may have researched industries and companies. You might have sent resumes to anything in the paper and faked the rest. Maybe you even networked your heart out. And finally after grueling hours of hard work and false leads, someone hired you. But that just gave you a new set of problems. What now? Keeping a job, not to mention succeeding in your career, is going to take a new set of skills.

The road between your entry-level position and a seat on the board of directors is a long and treacherous one. You know how much hard work it took to get your first job; now they actually expect you to be successful, a good investment or at least keep the job. No one said a word about that in any class you took or book you've read. Now what? This book is about just that—the "now what." You'll discover how to keep that hard-earned job, even get promoted or get a raise you'll so desperately need, and how and when to leave and move on to your next career destination.

Until now, most of your life has been spent figuring out how to survive school and possibly your family. If someone asked you to write a term paper right now, you'd be fully prepared. If someone asked you to do your chores, you'd know what to do and what kind of trouble you'd be in if you didn't get them done. You may hate 'em, but you know how to do them. But how do you do this new job? Overnight you are supposed to turn into that productive member of society you've heard so much about. You report your first day and think, "Toto, I got a feeling we aren't in Kansas anymore." And you aren't.

Working full-time is a whole new world. When people pay you to do something, they have a different set of expectations than when you pay them tuition. There are different consequences when you are doing something for a living than when you are dealing with your family and friends, who pretty much have to put up with you.

Your first day of work is looming on the horizon. Your energy has been spent figuring out how to get the job, and your imagination has been dreaming about what it will be like to run the place. But the reality is you've got to figure out how to navigate in a brand-new world. You must be very brave.

Right off the bat, here are some things you can expect. You can count on having some lousy assignments and some great ones. You'll have some great mentors and supervisors; you'll also work for people that medical science wouldn't classify as human. Sometimes you'll really click with the people you work with, and sometimes you'll think you've been hired in an asylum. Morale at your company will be jubilant to suicidal. You'll get praised, ignored and yelled at, sometimes on the same day.

Wait! Before you flip out, remember that your new company wants you to succeed. They've probably interviewed a few people, and they decided that you are the one they want. They've seen something in you they like. They have confidence you can do the job, even if you don't right now. That's why they hired you. The company will start out on your side, if for no other reason than it saves them the trouble of going out, finding and training someone else.

Think of your new job as a trip to a strange country and think of this book as a travel guide with maps and planning tools to help you find your way, and understand the customs and manners of the place. You certainly don't want to look like a goofy tourist getting lost, offending everyone and eventually getting deported. Let this book help you figure out how to get from your entry-level job to your ultimate goal and look upon it as a map to point out some interesting things along the way. It will help you understand corporate cultures and provide a simple understanding of the written and unwritten laws and customs of business. With any luck, you will feel like a local and you'll confidently embark on a professional trip that will last for forty-five years.

Road Rule #1: *If everyone else is driving on the right side of the road, it is not a good idea to drive on the left, even if that's what you are used to.*

QUICK TIPS FOR YOUR FIRST DAY

FOR YOUR FIRST DAY, ASK YOURSELF WHAT THE PEOPLE WERE WEARING WHEN YOU INTERVIEWED. COME AS close to wearing something like that as you can. If your supervisor, the person who is going to be deciding what kinds of jobs to give you, was strictly white shirt and red tie, it's best to leave the Hawaiian shirts for the luau. And if your new boss was in jeans and a Nirvana T-shirt, and you show up wearing the three-piece suit, you'll begin to think you hear people muttering "What a stiff" when you walk past. You'll be right. If in doubt, err on the side of slightly overdressing, then people might think you are classy. Over time you can casual-down. Even in a pretty casual place, if you dress for play every day, don't be surprised if people don't treat you like a grown-up.

Road Rule #2: *Don't worry if people pay no attention to you.*

They are in the middle of a regular day. Your arrival, as momentous as it feels to you, is probably just one more thing they have to get around to today.

Road Rule #3: *When in doubt, ask for personnel.*

They will give you tons of papers to sign. You'll have to figure out what insurance to take and what to have withheld for taxes; find out when payday is and where you should sit. Get a copy of the employee handbook and read it over. Personnel gets you on the payroll, so go find them.

Road Rule #4: *Introduce yourself to the receptionist and the mail room staff.*

Surprisingly, these people actually do want to know you and what you do, even if no one else seems to. They've got to get you the mail and put through your calls, so they care. Also, if they know who you are right away, you can get the all-important call from your folks to see how you are doing.

Road Rule #5: *Don't just sit there.*

Take some initiative and volunteer for something. Probably after personnel has had their way with you, they'll drop you off at your work space, and you will be totally alone and feeling useless. Don't get busted sitting at your desk making a paper-clip chain. Ask anyone and everyone if there is anything you can do to help them. Be prepared to lick stamps and alphabetize cards if that's what will be helpful. Sooner or later someone will remember they've hired you and start you off on your job.

Road Rule #6: *Try to get someone to go to lunch with you.*

Don't expect this to actually happen, but you should try. Ask whomever you meet around 11 A.M. if they have lunch plans and if you can join them. If anyone actually asks you to lunch, this is a miracle. So cancel your plans to meet your best friend. No one may ask you again for some time.

Road Rule #7: *Accept every task as if it were what you've been waiting to do your whole life.*

A little enthusiasm at the beginning goes a long way with people. They might not have planned anything for you to do yet, so they'll give you something easy to fill up your time. You'll eventually get to do the job you were hired to do, so don't worry about it yet.

Road Rule #8: *Introduce yourself to anyone who makes eye contact.*

Friendliness. Someone has got to start it. In most offices people see unfamiliar faces all the time. They don't know if you are a vendor, a visiting relative or a temp, all of whom everyone avoids talking to if they can. You are the new kid on the block, so behave as if you are someone people will want to meet. Take a deep breath and introduce yourself to someone.

Road Rule #9: *Don't ask to go home early.*

Even if you haven't done anything all day. Even if your supervisor forgot you were starting today and took the day off. Even if they are acting like you've come to read the gas meter. Everyone wants to think you can't wait to start working, and if you try to leave them, you'll hurt their feelings. Fill your time. Ask to see the company's annual report. Read any memos lying around. Go say "hello" to all the people you may have met during your interview process. Ask someone at the photocopier and fax machines to show you how they work. Find out how to use the phone and practice putting your mother on hold. Make someone teach you voice mail, electronic mail and any other kind of mail they have. Get lovely office supplies and organize them. This may be the last quiet day you'll have.

CHAPTER 1

WHAT Is an Entry-Level Job Anyway?

YOU KNOW THAT ADVERTISING AGENCY ON *MELROSE PLACE*, WHERE SOMETIMES THEY THINK UP COOL IDEAS and have lunch at neat places with clients, but mostly they try to destroy each other's lives? It's not like that. You know how on *Murphy Brown* they all sit around that table, drink coffee, toss ideas around and are really funny? It's not like that. Or even *Star Trek*, where whenever they get together there is going to be excitement and a chance to save the Federation from doom? Nope, not like that, either.

You and your entry-level job might be there on *Melrose Place, Murphy Brown* and even *Star Trek*. But you are, as they say in the acting profession, atmosphere. You are the person with your head buried in some papers when Heather Locklear storms to her office to hatch another hateful plot. You are the guy back at the file cabinet who only turns around to stare when Murphy gets riled up. If you aren't careful, you are the starship ensign with a couple of lines who you know will get killed off in the first half hour of the show. But your death will leave important clues for others.

Road Rule #10: *Don't let your ego be bigger than your current resume.*

No matter how smart you are, what school you went to or how much people like you, you are not the star of this show. In an entry-level job, you are a bit player, that poor actor walking deliberately across the screen, hoping someone will notice that she's even in the scene. But take heart. They give awards for supporting performances. People do notice good work. The company must think that what you do is important or they wouldn't be paying anyone to do it. And the bit parts are how you get to the starring roles. While your name may not be on the marquee yet, you can be the star of your own career.

Road Rule #11: *It will take more than eighteen months before they let you run the place.*

Entry-level jobs are usually beneath you, or at least they feel that way. Mostly you have to do work that requires a lot more patience than education. You'll fax stuff, you'll type stuff. They'll very likely make you file and take phone messages. You are probably some sort of assistant, which means they "think" and you "do."

You have lots of smarts and lots to contribute. But all those great theories you learned in school will only get attention from the big dogs after you've been able to prove you can put together flawless travel arrangements. You will have to prove that you can do the "little things" well before you get the really juicy assignments. Take a deep breath and make the photocopier your friend. You'll be following someone else to the door telling them where to go and what to do when they get there. They get to go off and be brilliant, and you get to clean up the conference room. Sometimes you'll stay up all night researching and putting all their concepts together.

> **Road Rule #12:** *The only thing you'll be asked to manage will be your expectations.*

All entry-level jobs are like this, so remember you are not alone. Unless you have entered a very specialized field, this idiot stuff is the kind of thing you'll be asked to do. And even if you are one of three psychothermal biomedical nuclear physical engineers in the world, if you are the new guy, they'll probably make you file too! No matter how brilliantly you passed your business courses, the only thing you will be called upon to manage at first will be your expectations.

> **Road Rule #13:** *You will always have way too much to do.*

Your first job description will probably be: "Do all the time-consuming and unrewarding stuff that has to be done, so that everyone else can do more of the cool stuff. If you really feel you must use your education and sharp, young mind, then think about how to do all this boring stuff better and faster so we can give you more of it and then we can do even more cool stuff."

Road Rule #14: *Do stupid things brilliantly.*

In that lies the first real challenge of your career. Do the boring stuff better and faster. Prove you can do that junk, and the doors begin to open. If you don't try to do this well, your career stops right here, and all you'll have to look forward to is more of the same. You may be ready, willing and able to discuss all the foreshadowing motifs in Hamlet, or do a prototype management/idea flowchart. But are you ready to take perfect phone messages? Ahh, there's the rub. And while you are thinking, "I am too smart to do this stupid stuff," remember: if you don't do it well, they will be thinking, "You aren't smart enough to even do this stupid stuff. I'm sure not going to assign you anything important."

Road Rule #15: *Master the basics.*

You are certainly able to hold complex and fascinating conversations in English. But when you first arrive in a foreign city, it's useful to learn a few simple phrases, like "please," "thank you" and "Where is the bathroom?" Mastering simple things can make your stay much more pleasant.

There is another payoff for mastering the basics. Business has changed dramatically in the last few years. When your folks started working, they measured success by how many assistants they had working for them. Now, the more assistants someone has, the more management wonders who's actually accomplishing the work. The economy has forced companies to do things in new ways. Many companies are eliminating most of the strictly clerical positions; everyone else is expected to perform a lot of that stuff and so are you. Since you are the entry-level person, you'll be asked to do more of it than most. All employees are called upon to do a variety of tasks, most of which no one really wants to do. Take comfort in knowing that no matter how far you rise in your career, you'll have lots of tasks assigned to you that make you wonder why they aren't someone else's responsibility. The job has not been invented yet that is not made up of lots of work that you just don't want to do. As it turns out, that's why you get paid for doing it. If it were all great fun, they'd find a way to make *you* pay.

These changes in business are not altogether a bad thing for you. The workers who are going to succeed in the next millennium are those who are able to be self-sufficient. The work force is leveling out. People in middle-management are becoming the blacksmiths of business: charming and picturesque, but no one really needs them. Power and influence are no longer measured in corner offices and multiple assistants. The ability to just get things done efficiently and independently is the most important skill to have for the new work force. Companies are busy flattening the organization, taking out all those junior and middle-management jobs. They are creating ways for people to work from many places and work more independently. Every computer program you have to slave over, every trick you learn for makin' copies will actually make you a more valuable employee for the future.

Road Rule #16: *If this work weren't important,*
they wouldn't pay you to do it.

Finally, if you've done the work yourself, how much better will you be able to manage others who do it? You can't become the tour guide until you've been the tourist. If you can get on the phone and do research for yourself, make your plane reservations, order the lunch and still be brilliant at the meeting, you might just be running the place soon.

CHAPTER 2
WHY Bother?

WHEN YOU ARRIVE IN A NEW CITY OR A NEW COUNTRY, THE FIRST THING YOU'VE GOT TO DO IS NAVIgate through a strange airport. You have to find the baggage claim, wait for your bags, figure out where to get transportation. This can be complicated and confusing. Imagine that you've finally arrived at Orly Airport in Paris. You don't understand the signs, everyone is speaking a strange language, and they've lost one of your bags. So what do you do? If you decide to turn around and go home, you've missed a great city. Your impression of France will be a little skewed, too. You've got to get through your first job to enjoy a career, just as you've got to get through the madhouse at Orly to sip red wine at a sidewalk cafe and wear a silly beret.

Road Rule #17: *Entry-level positions are rarely fascinating.*

You've begun to climb the ladder of your career. It's a long climb. In fact, it takes about forty-five years before they'll let you out again. By then you'll probably just want to sit in an easy chair and be cranky about the remote control! Your working life will take up most of the rest of the time you've got on earth. The steps you take and the lessons you learn now can make the rest of the climb a whole lot easier. That's what entry-level jobs are for: to learn this stuff.

How well you do at your first job and the lessons you learn there are going to make a difference in your work habits and your ability to get ahead for the next forty-five years. If you start a new job and give up on it in the first few weeks because you think you know how to do all this stuff, you are going to have to start your first job all over again. Lots of people start their first job several times before they get it right. But unlike dating, if you don't take the time to really get to know what this is about, it will cost you a lot more than dinner and a movie. It's a commitment thing. (OK, how many men just lost their breath for a second?) Here's something creepy to think about: They say you marry the same person over and over again if you don't learn your lessons from the first miserable marriage. The same is true in the working world. You go from one miserable entry-level job to another if you don't figure it out. You've got to challenge yourself to learn from every manager, good and bad, every assignment, simple or complex, and every new situation that comes your way. That's how you learn to navigate a career.

So why work so hard to keep your first job? The most practical reason is that it is the best path to the next and hopefully better job. If you can't stick, it makes it harder to get another job. If your resume is one six-month stint after another, most recruiters are going to figure the trouble is with you, not the twenty jobs you've had. Common denominator stuff. And if you are going to be a denominator, for heaven's sake, don't be a common one! It is always easier to get a new job when you have an old job. You don't have as much financial pressure, and a potential employer thinks at least someone is willing to put up with you, so they'll be more likely to give you a shot. Interviewers can smell defeat and desperation on you. It can make a difference in getting a better job if they can see you are moving on to something instead of running away.

The work they give you in an entry-level position may not seem challenging, but it is an excellent source of information. You may have been answering the phone and giving accurate messages since you were six years old. But there's a lot to learn in these messages. You may think typing is for a secretarial pool, not for someone with your expensive education. But there may be some good reading in that stuff you are typing, more current and relevant business information than any book you read for a class. When you have to make thirty photocopies of that business plan, you can stare at the counter and be mesmerized by the rhythm of the machine, or you can read a hot-off-the-press business plan and analyze it. OK, there is no getting around the not-so-enlightening stuff like organizing a lunch. Yes, it's tedious. But if they didn't need someone to do it, they might not have needed to hire you. You might as well do it well.

Unfortunately the only way out of any entry-level job is to get through it. If you don't learn everything you can from your first job, you are condemned to live it over and over again. If you don't move up, you just move sideways. If you sign up for the gym every six months, but only go the first few weeks, you don't get fit. The same is true for your career. In order to get anywhere, you've got to stay in the same place long enough to develop relationships, skills, confidence and an understanding of your profession. You know you can do all this stuff, but your first job is about proving that you can do it.

Road Rule #18: *The only way out of entry-level jobs is to succeed at one.*

You can change ladders; lots of people do. Most people change careers several times during their work life. This is a good thing. It means you are changing and growing. What you like to do and what you do well should keep expanding. Remind yourself when you get frustrated that this won't be the only job you'll have, it's just the job you've got for now. Most entry-level jobs are pretty much the same. You can run but you can't hide. Think of it as the cough medicine of life: it tastes pretty rotten, but it's supposed to be good for you.

Road Rule #19: *You can learn a lot from the crummiest jobs.*

There is lots you can learn even from the worst job, lowest position and meanest environment. You can learn how the business works and how to deal with people and procedures. You'll learn strategies about getting along and getting attention. Of course, if you are being harassed or truly misused, you need to do something about it, up to and including getting out and starting again. But if you can do it, give your first job at least ten months. This book will help you to get through it, hopefully rise from it, or at the very least, survive it!

Road Rule #20: *They pay you to do the stuff you already know how to do.*

Here's the deal. School is where you pay them to learn, work is where they pay you. But you can still learn and get paid for it, too, if you take the time to see what's there. No one will stand up and tell you what you need to learn. No, they make it hard. You have to look for it. There's plenty to learn, too. Open your eyes and ears. You'll be amazed.

CHAPTER **3** F**IRST Impressions**

Y OU CAN'T JUDGE A BOOK BY ITS COVER, BUT THAT
DOESN'T KEEP PEOPLE FROM TRYING. THOSE FIRST
shallow impressions of you may be what you have to overcome for the rest of your job life. Your coworkers and
managers will watch you more closely now than they ever
will again. You are like a thriller they've never read before.
Everything about you is a clue. How you look and act your
first weeks on the job will have more to do with what
people think of you than anything you actually accomplish.
Cheap, unfair, and true.

Road Rule #21: *Don't be the first to arrive or the
last one to leave.*

Different companies have different rhythms. Discovering
when everything happens and when nothing happens is
going to help you be in the right place at the right time.
Just because they told you the hours are nine to five during
the interview, don't believe it. Some companies start bright
and early, and some tend to stay late. Don't miss these

times; this is when work is informal, coworkers bond, ideas are exchanged and relationships develop. If a company starts early and you come in at 9 A.M., you won't be there to get good assignments. If a company stays late, but you arrive at the break of dawn, you'll be in for some long days. When everything breaks open at 4:30, they'll need you to stay until the unofficial day ends at 9 P.M. At the same time, if you want some quiet time in the office to catch up, it's best to be there when everyone else isn't. You don't have to be the first to arrive and the last to leave every day, but you shouldn't be the last to arrive and the first to leave either. Find a happy medium.

Often there is a lunch time. It's not necessarily at noon. If you go out at noon, and most of the other people don't go until 1 P.M., they will all be wondering where you are for an hour. When you get back, you'll have a hard time getting much done, because you are all alone . . . and that's so sad. It's like going shopping in Spain at 1 P.M. You may be ready to buy, but the entire country is taking a nap. Make sure that people don't do lunch on shifts. Someone may expect you to answer the phones while they eat. If you aren't there and the phones go nuts, unhappiness ensues. Figure out the rhythm of the company so you can make it work for you.

Road Rule #22: *There is always a corporate culture.*

There is this strange, nebulous thing called a corporate culture. Every place has one. It's hard to see, but it's important to understand. It defines what the group is like and how they behave with each other. Some places are conserva-

WORK SHEET #1

*The Starting Off on the Right Foot
and in the Right Shoes Work Sheet*

The old adage "You can't change the rules unless you know how to play the game" is especially true when you are starting out with a company. You'll want to spend your first months proving what a fine choice they made by hiring you. You don't want to spend that time making up for the dumb stuff you did right off the bat. "I didn't know" will be small comfort while you eat lunch alone every day for thirty years.

Here are some questions you might ask yourself your first few weeks on the job:

Is my tie:

    A) just like the waiter's in that dive bar I was in yesterday?
    B) very much like the guy's who has the job that my boss wants?
    C) always good for a laugh?
    D) the only one being worn in my department?

Would my supervisor wear a skirt this style:

    A) while doing the laundry?
    B) when she is trying to impress her client?
    C) when hell freezes over?
    D) only when her boyfriend Ernst returns from three months at sea?

I could also wear the clothes I'm wearing at the office:

    A) to repair my car?
    B) to an interview for a new job?
    C) to the coolest night club in town?
    D) to the beach in case I'm fired before noon?

I arrive at work:

    A) about the time everyone in the group has already had one cup of coffee too many?

    B) not much earlier or later than anyone else?

    C) in time to watch the sun rise, all alone?

    D) when my supervisor is looking at the clock, and then at me, then the clock?

Do I leave work:

    A) and say good night to everyone else and always get an elevator all to myself?

    B) about five minutes after my boss leaves?

    C) within a millisecond of quitting time? Do I get my coat and stuff ready to go fifteen minutes early, so I won't be late?

    D) in time to watch the sun come up, all alone?

When I have some downtime do I:

    A) call my best friend and trash all my other friends for an hour or so?

    B) ask everybody I see if I can help them with anything, or ask questions?

    C) stare at a blank computer screen and try to look intense?

    D) go from my desk to the coffee machine to the bathroom again and again, pausing only to look at the clock?

Do I love the radio in my office because:

    A) I can hear it from the men's room?

    B) it is nice when I'm working late?

    C) it is the only one in the entire office?

    D) I can't hear the phone ring with the earphones on?

If you've answered anything but "B" it might be best not to count on that lovely paycheck much longer.

tive and strive to be as different from actual humans as possible. They wear suits. They bow and scrape, paying careful attention to title and procedures. The funniest story in the world will only receive an icy stare. Other workplaces seem so relaxed you are amazed no one comes to work in their pj's. Hilarity seems to be the order of the day. But even in these places people are very serious about the work. Hopefully you have chosen a work environment and culture that you can live with. If the culture of your new company feels more like a culture you'd only want to see in a petri dish, then think of your time there as a science experiment. But don't think they'll change the culture for you. Pay attention to what is sacred behavior, the things that are *always* done, or simply *never* done. It's harder to spot sacred behaviors in a casual environment, but they are there. Don't blaspheme in the house of your paycheck.

Road Rule #23: *Act, think and dress like the job you want, not the one you have.*

Your first month on the job is a blank slate. Everything you do after the first five minutes is evidence about who you are and what kind of worker they expect you to be. Even the most open-minded person can't help gathering evidence about who you are. If you walked into your dorm, and your new roommate was listening to a soundtrack of *The Sound of Music* and you are strictly Bon Jovi, it would take a lot for you to believe that the roomy from hell might be all right after all. It would be awhile before you would choose to spend time with this person. Starting a new job is the same. This is all about being someone who appears to be someone everyone else there wants to work with.

People make snap judgments, and they change their minds very slowly.

This is not to suggest that you should take your personality and throw it away. Keep your sense of humor, heaven knows you'll need it. Exercise your whimsy. Hold tight to your sense of fair play and justice. But use them in the appropriate places at the appropriate times. You must be yourself, but sometimes you might need to be your most practical self, your most serious self or your most understanding self. There will be plenty of time to show everyone what a fascinating and multifaceted individual you are, but if you blow it now you'll never get the chance. They probably saw some of the real you in the interview and are looking forward to working with that person. Prove to your company that you "get" them. After you do, they'll give you the opportunity to show them your charm and your offbeat sensibilities. Sure, you can learn these lessons over time, but the longer you take to learn them, the harder it will be to prove you can be an important part of the team.

CHAPTER 4
YOU'VE Got the Look!

YOUR APPEARANCE
AND WHY IT MATTERS

REMEMBER HOW IN JUNIOR HIGH, YOU JUST HAD TO, HAD TO, HAD TO HAVE THE "RIGHT" TENNIS SHOES, shirt, jeans? And remember your mortification if you didn't? As horrid as this sounds, it's time to get back in touch with that pimply adolescent.

You were so stubborn about this stuff then because you believed that people were judging you by your ability to fit in. In college, you outgrew that and learned that those superficial judgments were just that—superficial. And you were right. But even in college, there was a costume that you and your tribe wore. They may have been secondhand clothes or team sweatshirts, but they told people something about who you were. The problem is, people are going to make superficial judgments about you all the time, just the way you make them about others!

The principal difference between dressing appropriately now and when you were thirteen is that now it can translate into cash, or the lack of it. Raises and, more important, promotions, can happen or not happen based on your costume. Here are some practical reasons to pay attention to appearance in order to help you swallow this bitter pill.

Road Rule #24: *Most companies don't have a good imagination.*

They say you should dress like the job you want. It's true. If they can't picture you anyplace but the mail room, they'll never put you anywhere but the mail room! Look around. What are the big dogs wearing? What are the middle dogs wearing? You might not have an Armani budget, but you'll never have one if you don't wear budget Armani. When you look like that buttoned-up professional, they'll start to believe it. The weird part is, you'll start to believe it too!

Road Rule #25: *Don't wear heels higher than your ambition.*

Those marvelous shoes that you got for such a bargain may look great, but by 3 P.M., you could be limping around the office like a wounded animal. You have a long hard day ahead of you, so make sure you don't spend it obsessing about being immobile in that groovy but constrictive jacket, or tugging at your shirt.

Road Rule #26: *You are representing the company all day long.*

There are clients and vendors in and out of the office all day. The way each employee dresses will say a lot to these folks about what kind of place they are doing business with. Do you think anyone would want to do business with a Dead Head? What about that big inner-sanctum meeting someone may invite you to on a whim? They'll pull that precious invitation right out of your black-nail-polished fingers if you look like you pulled an all-nighter in your clothes. This is business, and the company needs to show it respects and understands its customers.

Road Rule #27: *Professional dress reflects a professional person.*

The kind of employee everyone wants working for them is the one who is paying attention to the details. Taking care not to wear the shirt with the big gravy stain in the middle says you notice things. Everyone accidentally wears one blue sock and one black sock sometimes. But if they can't trust you to button your shirt correctly half the time, are they going to trust you with the company books? Unless you've gotten a job as Albert Einstein, the rumpled eccentric look probably won't work for you.

Road Rule #28: *Show them you are taking this seriously.*

If you look like you are an escapee from the playground, they'll treat you like one. You want to be taken seriously? Act like it. (Oh my God, I sound like my parents! Could they have been right?) The first step in "acting like it" is getting dressed in the morning. If you dress like a disco princess, they'll believe that's what's important to you and stop wasting their time on you. Look like you mean business.

FASHION ALTERNATIVES FOR THOSE WHO JUST CAN'T BEAR IT

- The more conservative your dress or suit has to be, the funkier jewelry or tie you can wear. (No nude girlies on the tie no matter how Brooks Brothers the suit.)

- If you are wearing suit pants, don't forget that some great socks can offer a peek at who you really are.

- Spend money on a trendy chic haircut, although I wouldn't shave "Capitalism Sucks" in my scalp, no matter how trendy.

- Hats. You don't wear them in the office; but on the way to and from the place, you can scream "I am Me!" to the world with the right hat.

- Silly underwear. A conservative work environment is just what trashy underwear was invented for.

- The weekend. It always comes, thank God!

CHAPTER 5

YOU and Your Boss

SEE, IT'S LIKE THIS. WHEN YOU STARTED THEY ASSIGNED YOU TO SOMEONE WHO IS SUPPOSED TO MAKE SURE that the company is getting their money's worth from you. This person decides what you have to do and what you don't get to do. This all-powerful person decides if you get promoted, a raise or the boot. They get to tell you when you mess up and if they think of it, tell you when you have done good work. They aren't delighted that you can sit up, don't spit milk and sleep through the night like your parents are. They don't think it's funny when you zone out and completely lose track of conversations or forget to wear your shoes like your friends do. They are the boss. They don't have to.

Road Rule #29: *Understand what motivates your boss.*

This is what your supervisor is thinking: "When I started my first job, I worked really really hard, had perfect attendance, asked very smart questions from time to time, but no one really trained me. By golly, I went out there and just did it. I knew what to do; it's just common sense. Initiative and perseverance got me promoted. And I was in that first job for a long time, really did two jobs at once. So what is their hurry to get promoted? They haven't paid their dues yet." Yeah right, and snow was whiter then, too.

Road Rule #30: *Your boss won't be perfect.*

No one has promised you a boss who is any good at supervision, delegation or training. In fact, you may find you are working for someone who has never managed anyone before. If you get one that has any experience and is any good at supervision, consider yourself lucky. Anyone who has never supervised before is pretty sure she could do it well. She will be kind and understanding. She thinks she will explain everything that has to be done with patience and care. She thinks she will be the friend of the staff. She thinks that when she is in charge everyone will be challenged, have fun and get a nice big raise. The trouble is, the employees keep showing up and ruining the fantasy. Managing is a great concept, but not an easy reality.

Frankly, most managers just aren't very good at it or have some gaping flaws. If your new manager really doesn't know how to do it, hopefully someone will figure it out and fix the situation. In the meantime, you have to spend your days with this person. You can't change your boss. You will have to live with each thing he does that you know you could have done better. You'll be required to put up with his moods and his mishandling of things. Sometimes he'll yell before he listens to your side of the story, if he listens at all. Some supervisors are great at it; most seem to be just OK at best. But what if they are right? What if they are doing exactly what is expected of them? After all, they've been there longer than you. And someone decided they had what it takes and made them the boss.

Road Rule #31: *Don't react; develop a strategy.*

The best you can do is to try to understand what motivates your new boss and develop some tactics for making the best of the situation. It's worth it to try. Dealing well with good and bad supervision is an important business tool. If you allow yourself to obsess about your manager, and use that as a reason for not doing great work yourself, you are only messing up your own life. You've got to learn to work with lots of people. The trouble with work is there are so many people there to challenge your sense of how everything should go. There are lots of bad managers out there, so you'll be meeting this challenge over and over again in your career. It only stops when you become someone else's bad boss!

Bosses come in lots of types. Take heart and take warning: a good or bad boss never has made or broken anyone's career. You alone can do that. Don't let yourself blame them for your failure. Then you have the right to congratulate yourself for your success.

Road Rule #32: *Don't smirk, even when they deserve it.*

So what do you do if your boss should not be allowed in the same room with anything but single-celled organisms? Whining is annoying and holding your breath only works if you are refusing to eat peas. You can't change her. So how do you survive? If you step back and figure out what makes your boss tick, you can develop a strategy for making the most out of working for her.

THE "HYPER-CONTROL FREAK" BOSS

If you feel you are being monitored every minute of the day and you can't even take a break without having it pointed out how you could do that better, you have a hyper-control freak for a boss. He will tell you how to do everything, from sharpening your pencil to turning off the desk light at the end of the day. In fact, he'll tell you twice. The hyper-controlling boss will want to see everything you produce. He will give you assignments in bits and pieces. You thought your parents told you what to do all the time; in comparison, the hyper-controlling boss makes your parents seem like disinterested bystanders.

The first thing you want to do is understand what motivates a hyper-controller. It isn't power. It isn't because they think you are stupid. It's fear. They are so afraid something will go wrong and they'll get blamed for it. They have a tendency to overcompensate all over you.

THE BAD NEWS

You will not be trusted to do anything on your own, not for a long time. You'll be second-guessed with every move. And you may have trouble getting the big picture from them, because they will dole out work a teaspoon at a time. You'll have lots of trouble getting any assignment that a fifth-grader couldn't handle. They will be checking on what you are doing so often you won't have time to do anything at all. And you will probably have to prove that you can do the same stupid thing over and over and over again before you get a chance at anything new. Stomping, muttering and holding your breath won't make it better. You'd better have a plan.

WHAT YOU CAN DO

After you've been there for a little bit, you can figure out that thing they always ask you for. Start to give it to them before they ask. Try to get ahead of their fears. If you know they want a status report every Friday at 9 A.M., try to get it for them Thursday late afternoon. If they always ask for the source of information, tell them before they get the chance to ask. To get a better picture of how your work fits in to the big picture, you'll need to ask this person lots of questions. If you think fast, after a while you can anticipate her every move, know more than she's thought to ask and bring the cookies. Keeping one step ahead of this sort of boss is useful. This disorients her. That's your chance to move in and get some respect. If you are more in control than she is, she'll start to relax. Then and only then will you start to develop some trust.

THE GOOD NEWS

You will learn more about how to do it right from this kind of manager than you ever will again. You'll understand the fine points of every step in the process. You'll learn to anticipate questions, and this leads to great work. Pay attention, because being meticulous has gotten this person ahead. It always does. You'll be able to outthink and outplan the best of them, because you've had to develop the discipline to do it. If God is in the details, this manager is the Pope. Don't worry, these guys seem crazy. They will be so relieved to have someone they can count on that they become amazing mentors for someone they trust.

THE "HANDS OFF" BOSS

Your new boss is someone you see from time to time as her office door closes behind her. If you saw her face-to-face, you would have to struggle to remember where you've seen her before. The face seems familiar . . . You've got a boss who is so hands-off she is invisible. This person gives you an assignment and is never seen again until the work is due, is wrong or is perfect. She isn't there to answer questions. She isn't there to check over what you've done. When you do actually find her to ask for some guidance, she'll look at you like you are the irritating younger sibling. She isn't in this biz to manage or mentor you, but to do her own thing.

THE BAD NEWS

Hands-off bosses may be motivated by the fact that they are psychotically busy. They have so much to do that they put blinders on to get it done, and you and your problems are out of their line of vision. You were hired to do the two jobs they just don't have time to do anymore, and then someone gave them three more jobs to do. In fact, they may physically be out of town a lot.

Even though you don't know how to do your job, they

expect you to do it, even if they won't have the time to stop and explain anything to you. What instructions you do get will be less than half of what you need to know in order to do the job well. School is definitely out, so it's going to be up to you to learn your own lessons, and learn them fast. They probably won't be very good at giving you feedback either, unless you've done it wrong. They won't pay much attention to whether you are doing a good job or not. When these people became managers, they knew the title implied more responsibility and more money. That actual managing might be required has never crossed their minds.

WHAT YOU CAN DO

The first thing to do is to find someone friendly who has had this job before or someone who is doing it now. Buy him lunch. Buy him drinks. Buy Cliff Notes from him. It is worth the investment. He can tell you what is expected of you. Second, be fast on your feet with questions for your manager and be ready to reel them off when she gives you an assignment. Have questions ready when you see your manager fly by on the way to the elevator; follow her down in the elevator if you have to. She won't remind you to do something twice, so get yourself a little notebook to keep yourself reminded. If you get any instruction at all, you'll only get it once, so you'd better make the most of it. You won't see her again until the spring.

Don't be shy, don't hesitate. Risk stupid questions if you must, but strike when she is around. Another tactic is to find the time when she will be the most open to your questions. If she gets to work early, get there early too. Find the time of the day that she is the most relaxed, and then pounce, but be sure to pounce. Be fearless. Be forward. This is your one chance.

Because she won't give you feedback, learn to acknowledge yourself for every little thing you do. Decide that what goes unnoticed must have been done perfectly. If it wasn't perfect, you would have heard about it. Pat yourself on the back and toot your horn around the office a little from time to time. More important, find a way of letting your boss know how marvelous you are. Send her a weekly note about what you've accomplished or what you are about to do. Say "Hey, we made the deadline for that big project" as she flies by. Don't think of this as kissing up; think of it as following up. That's an important thing to do.

THE GOOD NEWS

While figuring out how to do your job you will develop a great network in the company. Others will admire how resourceful you are. Because there isn't anyone there to tell you "how we've always done it," you can invent new and improved ways of making things happen. That can be fun. You'll be able to see the goal and go. Since there is no one there telling you not to, you'll get a chance to do things that others in your position won't get to try. If nothing else, people will take pity on you stumbling around in the dark and be nice to you.

THE "HIS JOB IS YOUR JOB AND YOUR JOB IS YOUR JOB" BOSS

You are wondering what on earth your boss does every day. Everything that happens in the department ends up on your desk. Congratulations, you have the "his job is your job, and your job is your job" boss. Sometimes he is in the office getting coffee or yacking it up with folks, but usually he is at lunch. He walks out every day at five, calm and relaxed, and you are about to have a stroke. If he's ever actually accomplished anything, you've never seen it. When you hear this person say "Sure, we'll take care of it," you know that "we" is really you. You slave, they saunter.

THE BAD NEWS

Sometimes people get the big bucks not to DO anything. They are paid to think great thoughts, and you are paid to get things done. This person may be paid to make sure things happen, possibly to strategize. At worst, you are working for the chairman's nephew. Comfort yourself by remembering if he were doing the work, you probably wouldn't have a job. The trouble is, he doesn't have a sense of how long things take or the volume of things that need to get done. He can really pile up stuff for you to do. Because he isn't doing it, he thinks there's plenty of time. And what's worse, he wants everything to happen quickly and magically, so he can go back to those great thoughts. But because he isn't actually doing the work, he doesn't understand why you don't "just get it done."

WHAT YOU CAN DO

Whatever it is that this manager is paid to do, or not do, it is important to keep focus on what you are paid to do. You are supposed to make sure stuff gets done. If this person is not producing what the company wants, sooner or later someone will do something about it. You aren't that someone. If you start keeping score with this kind of boss, you'll just go crazy. Don't let yourself slack off because you think your boss does. Guess who will get the ax first?

This is a boss who needs lots of feedback about you. It's going to be up to you to provide it. Make sure when you are given an assignment that you tell him how long it will take. Try always to say yes and add a simple "Well, a presentation this size takes about four hours to put together." This gives the manager some perspective about what he is really asking of you. Then ask for his help prioritizing all the things you've got on your desk that won't get done during those four hours. Don't just sit there and drown. Let him know what you are doing and if you are overloaded. Let him know what might not get done in time without some help. Don't be angry or desperate, just give him the facts. If you wait until you miss a deadline to talk about what's on your plate, he'll think you haven't been doing a thing. Unfair, but there you are.

THE GOOD NEWS

Pretty soon you'll be the person who knows everything there is to know. Because you've had to do more than your share, you'll know more than your share. You'll be the one everyone starts to go to for the answers. You'll have an understanding of how things work way beyond the scope of your job. In fact, you'll have a very good argument ready for why you should get the next promotion. Sure, you'll do lots of piddly things, but you'll also get a shot at doing things that others don't get to do for years. Make the most of it. People notice. They really do.

THE "WE ARE SUCH GOOD FRIENDS" BOSS

You work for the nicest person in the world. Teamwork, that's what this boss is all about. Yet, as you are standing at the counter asking for extra starch, you have an uneasy feeling, because you are working for the we-are-such-good-friends-that-I-know-you-won't-mind-picking-up-my-laundry boss. She invites you to her place for a party, and the next thing you know you are ironing the cocktail napkins. You attend your first client meeting, and she asks you to get coffee.

This boss really believes she is a great boss. She thinks everyone is one big happy family, doing their part. The problem is, she thinks of you as the baby of the family, and you want to grow up! She is very open with you and wants you to see her as a friend, not a boss. But with real friends you get to tell them to stick it in their ear when they ask you to do something you think is unreasonable. You also aren't counting on your friends for raises and promotions, just cheap gossip about your other friends. Bosses are not your friends, no matter how friendly they are. But don't tell this boss that.

THE BAD NEWS

Trouble is, this boss isn't good at drawing the lines between her work life and the rest of her life. While it's great to work for someone so nice, sometimes it's hard to tell what is an assignment and what is a friendly request. You'd better assume that they are all assignments, no matter how pleasantly they are presented to you. Also, because she is so nice, it's very hard for you to confront her in order to get the clarification you need. Broad hints don't work. This boss will be very protective of the idea of the happy team, much more than she will protect your individual needs. The worst thing you can do with a boss like this is to be angry and confrontational. It's time to be friendly and persuasive.

WHAT YOU CAN DO

The secret you need to know is, this boss wants to be liked, even loved. She likes to believe that we are all one big happy family. Conflict is very upsetting to her vision of life, and that makes it hard to stand up for yourself when you are taken advantage of. If what you are being asked to do is clearly personal, like exchanging her husband's underwear for a smaller size, you'll have to talk to her. Remind her you are happy to do whatever needs to be done for the job and the team. Point out the things that won't be getting done for the company while you take care of her errands. And if you have to, tell her you just aren't comfortable doing this. Don't leave it there, though. Offer to do something else in the office so she'll have time to take care of what you think is too personal.

Tread carefully; some of that crummy stuff they are asking you to do actually is part of an entry-level job. That's why this boss can be so confusing. Getting coffee in a meeting is in fact your job; so is faxing stuff and cleaning up after the meeting. Mowing her lawn and rotating her tires is not. You can sit around and feel demeaned, or you make a damn fine cup of coffee. Everyone responds to the person who does every lousy thing he has to do well. You may want to ignore or zip through this stuff because it's beneath you, but she'll be thinking if you can't even make lunch reservations well, why would she give you something more complicated to do? Oh, and be "busy" for the next couple of personal invitations! Say you are taking a class, or your agoraphobic auntie is visiting for a few days.

THE GOOD NEWS

This is the kind of boss who will really mentor you, stand up for you and help you along in the company. She will also make lots of decisions by committee, so you'll be involved in decision making while others at your level won't. This boss is open about information, so you'll know what is going on from a more senior perspective. Plus, she is a soft touch for a raise, if you've earned it!

THE "HE HAS NO LIFE SO WHY SHOULD YOU" BOSS

He lives in the office; he even keeps changes of clothes there. No one has ever seen him leaving the office. His family and friends have filmed a "Missing Persons" segment for *Unsolved Mysteries*. Does he have a sort of ghoulish coloring, like someone who's been buried alive? Bummer.

You are working for someone who has no life, why should you? He likes to give you a big complicated assignment at 4 P.M., and wants to see it by 9 A.M. But don't worry, you won't be at the office all alone. No, he'll be right there with you, struggling with something until he is bleary-eyed and the sun rises on another day of living hell.

You've got a workaholic on your hands, and you need a step program to help provide the cure. Just when you think you've gotten something done, he'll find a couple of other ways for you to try it. Before you can put your pencil down from one assignment, there will be another project with your name on it in his out box. He never wants to be done for the day. He doesn't want you to be either. These bosses are perfectionists. Nothing is ever perfect.

THE BAD NEWS

It is very likely this person has a martyr complex. He believes he is underloved and underappreciated, and he'll spend as much time as possible trying to prove it. By working tirelessly night and day and weekends, he believes he is heroic. Why do a one-page report on becoming a paperless office, when you could do a fifty-page report? This boss will keep going till he cracks, and he is going to take you down with him.

WHAT YOU CAN DO

Sympathize sympathize sympathize. By keeping you there, he is proving himself to you too. So show him that you "get it." Make sure you find ways of acknowledging him as the most pathetic person in the company (in a loving way, of course). He is enjoying being miserable; help him by feeling sorry for him. Then start offering to do things for him so he can go home. The poor baby. Help him to get out of there, so he can breathe the fresh air again. Having a life could start to become a habit. Eventually he'll start to pay you back, and start sending you home too. If you ever see him streamline a process, be sure to tell him how brilliant he is to do this. And you might want to mention something about how "senior management will never appreciate this," so he can feel comfortably martyred. If this doesn't work, after a couple of months tell him you are going to take a night class. That way at least you will get out of there one evening a week!

THE GOOD NEWS

Everyone else in the company will want you to work for them. They know you've gone to boot camp, and if you don't grouse too much, they'll chomp at the bit to get you. Anyone who has worked for this boss has the ability to hunker down and do the impossible, and that's what managers want. You'll develop the discipline to accomplish twice as much as anyone else. Also, every job you ever have after this one will feel like a vacation.

THE "ALL CRANKY ALL THE TIME" BOSS

It's a beautiful spring day, and she behaves like someone just shot her dog. Compliment her on a job well done, and she'll tell you that "it damn well better have been done well." When you tell her that you just won the lottery, she grumbles and says something warm and congratulatory like

"Yeah right, just my luck." Rain or shine, winter or summer, success or failure, you are working for someone who is all cranky, all the time. She may have smiled once, if she saw a car accident or something. But unless you trip on a rolling chair and break your leg in front of her, you can be sure she'll never smile at you.

Someone this cranky probably has no idea how bad it is to be around her. This is normal behavior for her. She comes at you with a hatchet, then wonders why you are so upset. She really thinks she just gave you a simple constructive adjustment. But you saw the veins throbbing in her neck and the steam coming from her eyes as she fingered that letter opener. People who are this ill-tempered are really convinced that no one will like them. So they get busy and don't like you first.

THE BAD NEWS

This person is a big honkin' drag to be around. She hates her life, and she hates the rest of humanity for being in her hateful life. People like this just aren't happy unless they are miserable. It's a lifestyle choice. And since you work for her, you get to be the object of the best of her anger. You don't do a perfect job, and it is an example of how the whole world is a cesspool. You get the job done well, and she hurries up and gets cranky about the next thing in the pipeline. Misery to her is like breathing to the rest of us, perfectly natural and constant. This one's hard to live with. It takes amazing patience, Teflon skin and lots of sugar, but you can do it.

WHAT YOU CAN DO

People who are this mean generally don't think anyone could possibly really like them. But if they are mean to you, at least they get to decide why you won't like them. But remember Pollyanna and that bad-ass aunt? Remember how Little Polly wore her down to a big lavender-perfumed mush ball? How? All those happy thoughts and that positive attitude stuff eventually rubbed off on the old auntie. I know this may seem sickening to you, but it actually works.

The trick is to like her anyway, and just keep liking her. We all know this. We've been taught from an early age in fairy tales that when you are kind to the ogre, it will come to your defense; and when you take the thorn from the lion's paw, it will purr like a kitten for you. Feel sorry for the mean and hateful ones, but dedicate yourself to being a little ray of sunshine in their gray lives. Never take the bad mood personally, and never give it back to them in kind. This part is hard, but if you defend them to their detractors, you build an amazing trust.

THE GOOD NEWS

Well, honestly, putting up with someone everyone else at the company probably hates won't do much for your career, but who needs raises and promotions? You are assured a place in heaven. If you are actually able to win this person over, and it does happen sometimes, she will be as loyal to you as a dog is to the person who rescued it from the pound. She will be your advocate at every turn and really help boost your career. Besides, being horrid back to her won't get you anything but as miserable as she is, so you might as well be nice. Actually, what often happens is that someone feels so sorry for you, and thinks you are such a lovely person, that you will be rescued. She will get you transferred to the warm bosom of another, much friendlier department.

Road Rule #33: *Plan first, react second.*

You are on a busy street corner in Rome. You stop and ask for directions to the Forum. They don't speak English. Screaming "Where is the lousy Forum?" louder and louder is not going to get you there. You'll be thinking how stupid everyone is, and they'll be thinking "ugly American." Try something else. Take out a map. Flip through your Italian/English dictionary. Cry. But do something.

It's a good idea whenever you have a conflict at work (and there will be plenty) to step back and develop a strategy. Being angry, frustrated and unhappy may have persuaded your folks to get you a car, but it won't do a thing at work, except make things worse. Sooner or later everyone finds she is working for someone who isn't so great or with whom she just doesn't jibe. Being emotional is understandable, but it won't help. Being mad can be personally satisfying but is very likely to backfire. Ignoring the situation won't change it. If your boss is great, congratulations, and be grateful. Even with a great boss, though, it can be hard to ask for what you want. So you need to decide what you want, how to say it and how to justify it.

Road Rule #34: *It is your responsibility to figure out how to get along with your boss.*

The first thing to do is step back and look at the situation as if you were giving someone else advice. If you weren't working for this person, and were just observing him, what would you be able to notice? What would you see that motivates him, moves him and wears him down? (If your boss is extra hateful, pretend that you are observing him caged in some zoo; it might give you pleasure.)

Overcoming troubles with your boss is possible. You can't change who he is; you can take command of *your* behavior and expectations. To do this, develop a strategy. Often it takes several tries, so if the first strategy doesn't work adjust it and try again.

Make sure you give your plan plenty of time to work. It took some time for your manager to get that way, it's going to take lots of time to get him to stop doing it to you. One shot, even one week won't do it. You get unemployment for twenty-eight weeks. Give your plan at least half that amount of time.

What you are doing now isn't working, so why keep doing it? Even if you are completely right, you will only be right and miserable. If you step back and find a new way to approach the person, you may break through. At the least you aren't being a doormat, you are participating in your own life! Don't ever forget it is more important for you to find a way to get along with your boss than it is for your boss to find a way to get along with you.

Road Rule #35: *The only person you have any lasting effect on is you.*

Working for some people can be a miserable experience

if you let it be. But these are only people, after all, and for most of us this is really only a job, not a world-changing endeavor. Keep your sense of humor and you can put up with a lot. Keep your sense of humanity, even for your managers, and it can be a comfort to you. You won't change them, you don't have to marry them, you just have to work for them for the time being. Something and someone better will come along. There is something worthwhile in even the creepiest boss. Keep perspective, and you'll be able to see it.

WORK SHEET # 2

The Getting Along with the Big Cheese Work Sheet

Answer these questions, and distill the answer to one sentence when possible. Be specific. Be realistic.

What are three things about my boss that I just can't stand?

_____

_____

_____

Study the above list very carefully. Are you studying it? Look it over one more time.
Now get over it.
Time for a strategy.

How do I want my boss to treat me?

_____

_____

Why is that important? (Your boss doesn't need to be your best friend or substitute parent.)

_____

_____

Does my boss treat anyone at all the way I want to be treated?   Y   N

If no: Put on a tough skin and don't take it so personally.
If yes: WHAT DO THOSE PEOPLE DO THAT I DON'T DO?

_____

_____

What are things I've seen or heard my boss praise in me or in others?
(If not praise, at least not grunt at.)

_____

_____

What are my boss's hot buttons? (What just burns her up, every time.)

_____

_____

What can I do to avoid pressing those buttons? (For God's sake, don't
make 'em mad.)

_____

_____

Why do I think my boss has this job? (Come on, you can come up with
something for this one if you try. It will tell you what the company values.)

_____

_____

What does my boss think that he/she is really good at?

_____

_____

*(This will give you a good clue about what the boss thinks is valuable in an
employee. We all think the stuff we are good at is the important stuff, and
the stuff we aren't good at doesn't really count.)*

What are three things I am good at, or I would like to try?

1 _____

2 _____

3 _____

Are any of these three things:
In the scope of the job I was hired to do?   Y   N
Valuable to my department?   Y   N
Valuable to my boss?   Y   N
Something I would trust to the new kid?   Y   N
Something someone is already being paid to do?   Y   N
(You've got to get three out of five yeses on the above. If not, reset your sights and make some new goals.)

Does my boss know what I'm good at and would like to do?   Y   N
("He should know if he's been paying attention" is NOT a yes answer.)
If no:
How will I tell him what I'd like to do?

_____

_____

If yes: How will I *show* them what I'd like to do?

_____

_____

If I were the boss, what would I need to see me do or hear me say to make things better?

SEE:_____
HEAR:_____

What are three things I'm going to do to make life better? (Keep in mind what the boss thinks is valuable, what they are paying you to do and your skills.)

1 _____

2 _____

3 _____

CHAPTER 6

THE Big, Stupid Mistakes

DURING THE FIRST WEEK OF MY VERY FIRST JOB, I NOTICED LOTS OF SIGNS AROUND THE COFFEE MACHINE telling us to make more coffee if we took the last of the pot. It seemed very important. I decided, after avoiding taking the last cup for a few days, to go ahead and make a pot of coffee. I filled up the machine with water, put coffee in the filter while thinking "What a good girl am I" and went back to my desk. Pretty soon someone came up to me and asked if I'd just made a pot of coffee. Certain I was about to be applauded as a fine member of the team, I said yes. "Well," he said, "next time, put the pot back under the machine. There is coffee all over the floor." Then they handed me a mop and gave me a look reserved for the worst of morons. After I'd cleaned up the mess, I sat at my desk and called myself names for hours. I was sure that I'd be fired by the end of the day. How could they even consider keeping someone as stupid as me? But I wasn't fired. Today, among my numerous other job skills is the ability to make a fine pot of coffee, and every drop goes into the pot, you can be sure.

Millions of tourist go to Cheers in Boston looking for Sam Malone, search the guidebooks to find Tara in Atlanta and ask for directions to Rick's American Cafe when they arrive in Casablanca. They may be embarrassed when they discover they have been duped by Hollywood but they don't usually get deported for it. I once got on a first-class train in Germany with a second-class ticket. The train was on the move by the time everyone discovered my mistake. The conductor was angry, I was embarrassed, and I was forced to get off the train before I got where I was trying to go.

Road Rule #36: *You are bound to blow it at least once.*

You are going to blunder. You are going to mess something up really badly. You'll forget to schedule a meeting. You'll send a memo with a gaping typo like "We want to fuckus on the end" instead of "focus." Something horrible is bound to happen eventually. If you believe you have to be perfect, you will be working under a lot of stress and you won't make it to age thirty.

Road Rule #37: *To err is human.*

Never making mistakes is not the goal. Never making the same kind of mistake twice is. If you don't use your spell check or have someone proof every memo after a gaff like that, you are asking for it. Try very hard to do everything perfectly, but give yourself a break. There is no capital punishment for forgetting to fax a letter or anything else that can and will go wrong.

Sometimes it really isn't your fault. Sometimes it is. If it is your fault, own it. If it isn't your fault, explain how you got into this mess, say what you might have done differently to keep the problem from happening again. If it is never your fault, you aren't being honest with yourself and no one will believe it.

When you do mess up, it's a fine line between overreaching and underreacting. If you inadvertently set the reception area on fire by hiding a lit cigarette in the drawer when the elevator opens and then ask "What's the big deal? It's just a little charring," you might try to care a little more. If you offer to wax someone's car for all eternity because you stapled the report in the wrong place, you might be overreacting just a tad. That fine line is where you need to walk all the time. Handling your mistakes well is how you live through them. But when in doubt, err on the side of eternal waxing.

Road Rule #38: *Everyone thinks they can do your job better than you.*

Just about everyone who has ever had your job thinks they did it flawlessly. It isn't true, by the way. Lots of people helped them, showed them how to do the job right and pulled them out of the quicksand when they fell in. They asked lots of stupid questions (the questions didn't seem stupid to them because they didn't know the answers). They even made some blunders they would prefer to forget. As you move up, you'll think you were better, smarter, faster on your feet than the poor sap who takes your place. What is mysterious to you now very quickly becomes common sense. Most people learn about common sense by making uncommon mistakes first.

ABSOLUTELY TRUE BOO-BOOS

You won't be alone. That day when you do something completely idiotic, remind yourself as you are banging your head on the wall and clutching your stomach that many have gone before you. Most of those people have gone on to lead productive careers, even if they had to change jobs to do it. Here is a collection of some true blunders. The names have been changed to protect the humiliated. Everyone you work with has a story like these. They just don't tell you.

Road Rule #39: *Know who you are talking to.*

A young account person at an advertising agency had a client named Stan A. and a boyfriend named Stan B. One day she was on the phone with her client when her second line rang. She asked the client if he could hold for a second to answer her second line. She hit a button on the phone, said hello, and the caller said "It's Stan . . ." She immediately said, "I can't talk to you right now, I'm on the other line with my client. Man, he's such a moron, I can barely stand it. What a creep." A long silence followed. You guessed it; she'd picked up the first line and just told her client what a moron he was. He laughed, but she was asked off the account a very short time later.

Any phone call you answer in the office may well be the chairman, or worse, the chairman's spouse. That blustering ass in the hall may well be the most important client or a potential new-business prospect in the company. Unfortunately clients get to be blustery because they have the money that pays everyone. The satisfaction of righteous indignation has a short life span. You don't have to be sincere, but be polite. They made up a word for sucking up and dealing with the jerks you meet at work. The word is *professional*.

Road Rule #40: *Success is in the details.*

A friend of mine moved to New York from a small town in the South and got his first job in a large corporation. He got a couple of new suits and a pair of zip-up shoes that were all the fashion in his small town. After a few months he decided to buy a second pair of shoes, and because he couldn't find those beige zip boots he'd been so fond of, he purchased a pair of simple wing tips. The first day he wore the new, more conservative wing tips, a senior vice-president, who had never spoken to him before, smiled at him and said, "Nice shoes, Steve." Steve looked down for the rest of the day and realized that those zip boots said more about how small-town he was than any drawl ever could. Despite all his earnest efforts, he had to overcome being the goofball with the stupid shoes!

The lousy thing about working is that there is always someone watching, paying attention and making judgments. You don't have to totally bury your personality and style underneath three pieces and sensible shoes. But you do want the primary judgments about you to be about how brilliant you are. Go ahead and wear zip boots. But be prepared to be extra brilliant and hard-working. Even then, if you can't quite get invited to that meeting or if the big promotion is eluding you, it might just be the shoes.

Road Rule #41: *"But nobody told me" won't wash.*

A business school graduate was hired as the assistant manager in a very nice jewelry store. In his second week, the owner showed him where the keys were, how the alarm worked, how to empty the cash register, how to use the safe and how to open and close the store. A few days later, the store owner decided to leave early and told the assistant that she would see him tomorrow. Late that evening the store owner got a call from the police telling her that the store was open. She raced downtown and happily found that everything was OK; by some miracle nothing had been stolen from the wide-open store. She locked up, set the alarm and went home. She decided to give the new assistant manager the benefit of the doubt. She figured that he was probably nervous and forgot to lock the door when he left. When she asked the assistant about it the next day, he told the store owner that no, he had not forgotten. No one had told him specifically to lock up that night, so he just went home at 5 P.M., as he had every other night. He hadn't thought a thing about leaving a jewelry store unlocked and unattended at night and didn't really see what the problem was now. If the employee had simply forgotten, he would have been given another shot. That he didn't have any common sense was unforgivable. He was reading the want ads that afternoon.

If you try to do a little more than you are asked, you'll be teacher's pet. If you see a fire in the hall, even if they passed you over for office fire marshal, you might want to at least mention it to someone. You can get burned, too, even if it isn't your job to grab the fire extinguisher. No one will ever be able to tell you every step that needs to be done. You are smart; you are expected to figure some stuff out all on your own.

Road Rule #42: *Honesty is the best policy.*

Many companies have a dinner policy. If you work after a certain hour in the evening, you are entitled to a reimbursement for having a working dinner. The key is, it has to be a working dinner. One young woman in a law firm decided that she worked pretty hard and while she didn't always work late, she should get that $15 dinner stipend. So she went to her dad's restaurant and got a blank check pad. At the end of two weeks, she turned in her expense report for ten dinners at $15 a piece. People wondered why she didn't get sick of hamburgers. Then they noticed that all the receipt numbers were in numerical order. That led them to look at when she signed out of the building at night. It was easy to see that she left before the time the company would reimburse for dinner. This woman didn't lose her job, but they talked to her about it and didn't pay for the phantom burgers. I wonder if she ever understood why she never got promoted?

If you get cheap with the company, they will get even cheaper with you. And brother they can be cheap! But this still doesn't make it OK for you to take more than your paycheck without their permission. Companies like to think of themselves as beneficent and generous, but they are always on the alert for someone who is taking advantage of them. This goes for the cheapest bastards in the free world. In fact, the cheaper they are, the more they are sure you are trying to cheat them. If you are as cheap with their money as Scrooge was with his, they are much more likely to give you that Christmas goose at the end of the year. But if you are entitled to it, by golly put the bill on that expense report and don't look back. Nobody ever got a prize for helping to support the company by paying for all their own business expenses.

Road Rule #43: *They are watching you!*

A young man was working as the personal assistant to an executive in a busy company. The young man was very excited that this job could be a big break for him, even if it was mostly administrative. There was exposure to the big dogs, and he knew that would be useful. But his coworkers noticed that the young man was on the phone an awful lot. He wasn't very eager to cover for people when they took breaks, and when folks came by, he'd put his calls on hold and look annoyed at the interruption.

Then the phone bill came. And there were several charges for four- and five-hour calls to Denmark. When the office manager wondered out loud what on earth these calls might be, her assistant, who never got support from the young man, was only too delighted to tell her that the young man's girlfriend was in Denmark for the summer. When confronted about where he had five uninterrupted hours in a day to make these calls, he replied with confidence, "Well, if my boss needs me to do something, I just put the call on hold till I'm done, so I'm working as hard as anyone."

Hey, we all have lives, but the company is not interested in paying for it. When you are at work, that's what you should be spending your time doing. If you think you have time for long personal calls you might be out of touch with what is expected of you. Get off the phone and find out what they are paying you to do. Also, when you waste the company's money like that, imagine wasting everyone's raises and bonuses, including yours. It all comes out of the same pot.

> **Road Rule #44:** *It doesn't matter what everyone else does.*

At the end of my friend's first week on her new job, a bunch of people went out to lunch at a Mexican restaurant. Someone thought it might be a good idea to have a round of margaritas. Then someone else thought that just one more round wouldn't hurt a bit. Of course why have two rounds when you could have three. Finally, some brilliant person realized that because everyone was buzzed, they might as well not go back to the office at all but just stay there and keep going. Everyone agreed that this was the only sensible thing to do. My friend, deferring to her more experienced coworkers, went right along with everyone else. The trouble was that everyone else had gotten up and called their manager or someone on their team and asked if it was OK. My friend didn't, and her supervisor, who didn't take long to figure out she was tossing them back with a certain bad element, had an assignment that he needed her to complete for the next day. When she staggered home that night, there was a message from her boss saying she needed to be in at 7 A.M. to get that assignment finished. She only kept her job because the crowd all walked into the boss's office and claimed it was their fault. But it took a long time for this woman to prove that she had any good judgment at all. It probably kept her back from a promotion for six months.

Everyone else may not come into the office until eleven in the morning. Everyone else may have a couple of drinks at lunch. Everyone else may wear jeans and plaid shirts every day. But if you stop and look around, you'll notice that there is no everyone else. There are a lot of people in at 9 A.M., and there are lots of people in suits. The one person you are accountable to is your supervisor. It's doing things the way she wants that's going to count. You can hang out and do what everyone else does after work if you want, but during the day it's best to make your manager the person you take your clues from. It's called managing up. Everyone else may buy you a round, but no one else is going to give you a raise.

ABSOLUTE NO-NOS

A new job can be like visiting a strange country. You are going along having a lovely time when suddenly everyone around you gasps and runs from the room. Oops! You have broken a sacred custom you didn't even know about. You have stepped on the all-holy corporate culture. Pleading ignorance of the customs won't help you; you've already offended everyone.

How do you avoid these ghastly faux pas? During the first few weeks on your job pay very careful attention to how people behave. Still, just because you heard some lowly toad tell the big cheese to stick it in his ear doesn't mean that you can or should. Wait it out for a few weeks and see if the toad is still around. It can take time to have someone deported.

All companies have a little different corporate culture. However, there are some customs of business that no one should break no matter what kind of place they are working for. Here are some of them.

Road Rule #45: *Never send mean, nasty and personal letters on company stationery.*

You can send a letter to your friends and family on the company stationery to prove to them that you really have a job. But never send a letter of complaint or personal inquiry on the company letterhead. When you do, the recipient will assume that you are representing the company in this correspondence. I know more than one person who has lost his job when someone called his boss to complain about a letter sent under the company letterhead. (Oh, and don't send resumes or cover letters on company stationary. The person you sent the resume to now knows that you steal office supplies.)

Road Rule #46: *Don't call in sick when you are really on vacation.*

You get caught; you just do. Everyone gets caught. This is not cowardice on my part, it is a fact of business. Unlike school, if you are out sick, you may well get called at home to find out where a file is or to be asked about a project. If you aren't home, they may worry that you're dead, but it's more likely they'll have suspicious thoughts. And your roommate will blow it, I promise. If that doesn't happen, you'll tell someone in the office, and they'll let it slip. Or everyone will wonder how you got that tan in the hospital. It happens every time. If you need time off, ask for it.

Everyone at the company has a life, places to go, people to see. Everyone gets some vacation time; that's what it's for.

Road Rule #47: *No cheating on time sheets and expense reports.*

Madness. No matter how you justify it, it's theft. You got a check on payday for all the work you did, and now you and the company are even. Trying to sneak a friend on a business trip and hiding the expenses seems like a harmless idea, but if you get caught, it won't be worth it. Padding your time sheet is the same thing. You put down hours you aren't working, you're stealing money. Your time sheet or expense report is an invoice. Sooner or later someone figures it out when you falsify it. And they won't be thinking how clever you were to try to get away with something. They'll be thinking about how they can't really trust you.

Road Rule #48: *Your long, long, long-distance calls should be on your personal bill.*

The same goes for hours of long-distance phone calls. They actually look at the bills, and if there are $50 worth of long-distance charges to your hometown on every bill, someone will put it all together. Most companies don't mind if you make an occasional and quick long-distance call, but not daily, and not hours and hours worth. Not only is the company paying your personal phone bill but they will wonder why you have so much free time on your hands. At best you lose trust and credibility; worse, it is a fireable offense.

Road Rule #49: *Avoid the "By God, I'm going to tell them what I really think of them" voice mail (or memo, or electronic mail).*

They have really done it this time. You won't take it, you are going to give them a piece of your mind. Very often when you give someone a piece of your mind, you have already lost your mind. No matter how steamed you are, don't blow now. Even if you know you are right, walk away. Give it forty-eight hours. If you are right, you won't be less right in two days. Write that very sharp note, but don't send it. Make your friends listen to what you are going to tell those lousy pigs (this is best done with lots of beers in a dark, crummy bar). If you still feel the same way a couple of days later, then go ahead and let it rip. But in the heat of the moment, you aren't going to see the whole picture very well. There may be more or even less to what you are mad about than you know. In the heat of the moment you aren't thinking about the possible consequences of your actions. Make sure you are willing to pay the price for telling someone off. Never say any more than "I'd like to speak to you when you have a chance" on a voice mail or e-mail. You can't take back a hysterical voice mail when you calm down. And getting a screaming voice mail only makes the recipient defensive and mad, so they'll never hear your point. Always have the showdown in person, but only when you can say what you really mean in a calm voice and can listen to the other person.

I have a friend who after a really bad day at work, goes home, drinks a few thousand bourbons and writes poison-pen e-mails to everyone he hates. This is a very satisfying evening after a long day at the office. Then he pours himself another drink and deletes them all. This is a smart businessman.

Road Rule #50: *Lunch hours are only sixty minutes long.*

I strongly urge you to get out of the office for lunch whenever you can. If you bring your lunch, then walk around the block or something, but get out and recuperate. If you are doing a good job, you'll need it.

On the other hand, usually in entry-level jobs, people cover for each other during breaks. Someone has to pick up the phone or fax that all-urgent fax, and someone has to be there to do it. If you are taking long and leisurely lunches, don't be surprised if you are really bugging your coworkers. Same goes for breaks. Your coworkers will not hesitate to complain bitterly about you if you leave them in the lurch. This annoys managers, and they get even. If you are taking advantage of breaks, please note that you are giving up any right you have to complain about being overworked. And complaining about being overworked is one of the joys of the job. An extra fifteen minutes at lunch aren't worth losing it.

Road Rule #51: *Never say "It's not my job."*

If someone has asked you to do something they must think that it's your job to do it. They may be right. So don't leap in with a big "Not me, pal!" If there is any way you can do what's been asked of you, do it. People like to hear "yes." Say it loudly and often, and you will be rewarded. Sometimes you are given work that they don't expect you to actually do; they just want you to help make sure it gets done. This, by the way, is a good thing; it's how you practice being a manager. If you are asked to make sure something is done, then be sure to follow up. If what you've been asked to do really really isn't your job and you don't know how to take care of it, you can give a "I think Susie's group does this, but I'll be glad to make sure she gets it." Notice how the word *no* does not appear in that sentence. As you go through your career, it is useful to find different ways to say no without ever quite saying it.

Road Rule #52: *Always follow up.*

One of the most common ways that people starting out blow it is by assuming everyone they work with is as dedicated and thorough as they are. Nothing will bug your manager more than if you constantly say "Gee, I gave it to him," or "I called them, I don't know what happened." If you've been asked to schedule a meeting, a lunch or make travel arrangements, the time it takes to confirm is nanoseconds in comparison to the hours of rage that your boss will have if they miss a meeting, can't get into the restaurant with the big client or can't get back to town. Flawless arrangement making makes brilliant careers. Same goes with anything that you pass on to someone else to take care of. You may have given the job to someone who is not as interested in your impressing your boss as you are. Never rest until you hear that it's all been taken care of. I know people who carry around notebooks with everything they've been given to do. Then call and call and call until the thing is done and they can cross it off the list. Because these people are so annoying to everyone, their work gets done first, just so people don't have to get all those darn calls. Just doing the task is only half the job. It's not done until it's done right.

W O R K S H E E T # 3

The I Am About to Make a Fool of Myself Work Sheet

Think about what you want to do. Answer yes or no to each statement.

My mom would yell at me if I did this _____
She would be right _____
I saw someone on court TV who had done this _____
My voice goes up two octaves and three decibels when I start to talk about this _____
If I do this, I'd better not tell anyone about it _____
This would make a good movie-of-the-week plot _____
This will show the lousy bastards _____
If I did this at my best friend's house, they would never speak to me again _____
My cousin in jail would think this is a good idea _____
I work hard. They owe me this _____
They didn't mean me when they said not to _____

If you said yes to any of the above, wait forty-eight hours before doing anything. Or make sure you've got really comfortable shoes to wear while standing in the unemployment line.

CHAPTER 7

THE Things No One Will Bother to Tell You

YOU'RE NO FOOL. NOBODY HAD TO TELL YOU THAT CHEERLEADERS AND JOCKS GET MORE DATES, OR good guys don't always win. But you probably had your heart broken first. Actually, I'll bet someone did try to tell you, or maybe you saw it in some movie. But you believed that they were ridiculous until you tried it and found out the hard way. Admit it, you put your hand on the hot stove once despite clear warnings. An important part of learning is doing it wrong first. So I'll try to tell you a few things, but you won't listen. No one ever does.

Road Rule #53: *All first jobs have a glass ceiling.*

Don't hurt your head. There is a glass ceiling in business. A glass ceiling is what your head keeps hitting as you are climbing the ladder of your career. You can't see exactly what it is, but no matter how hard you try, you can't seem to get past it to the next rung of the ladder. Look around your company. What may start out as a pretty mixed group can become more of one kind of person as you go up. See anyone of your gender or race up there at the top? You can only break through a glass ceiling if you know it's there. And sometimes you can't even then.

Road Rule #54: *It is hard to be taken seriously.*

There are other kinds of glass ceilings as you climb up the ladder. The first one you'll hit is the "little you" level. When you start out, you are the kid, everyone's little protégé. It's hard not to be seen as the kid no matter how hard you try. You can send a great proposal, and they'll think it's adorable. You can invent a new product, and they'll think it's precious. You can try putting gray hair at your temples and using a walker, and they'll think you are a little darling.

There are two ways out of or up from the little darling period. First: you can make sure you stop thinking of yourself as the kid. Never behave like the kid, and sooner or later your management will forget about it. There will be lots of new kids for them to treat like a puppy. The other way out is to go out and get another job after a year or so. Now you are the person with experience. The new company will believe you are a capable professional and, more important, you'll believe it of yourself.

Road Rule #55: *There will always be office politics.*

Put more than three people together with paychecks at stake, and there will be office politics. Even if the company claims it's not political, it is. It's just a different kind of politics from other companies. The game may be to be the slickest manipulator in the world or the nicest bastard who ever took a breath of life, but there is always a game. Sometimes companies call their political arena "culture." Corporate culture is really how we play nice together and still get ahead. It's what behavior is rewarded and what is punished. Just like Washington D.C., sometimes mudslinging, divisiveness and campaign dollars can get the votes. You gotta get the votes. However, it has been my experience that sooner or later the mudslingers end up covered with more of what they throw than the target. While an occasional "cover your butt" memo may be in order, your own actions are what will be judged, not how fast you can point a finger. More often than not, office politics take a long time to figure out. They are subtle, and there is a capriciousness to who's in and who's out. You'd better play very carefully. In fact try not to play at all. Even in the most political office, you don't want to be branded as being political.

Road Rule #56: *When the game gets dirty, play squeaky clean.*

The best way to proceed in a political company is to play your own game. It takes lots of know-how to win at someone else's. The more pejoratively political a place is, the smarter it is for you to be earnest, honest and only respond to direct information from the source and your own experience. Don't let gossip and innuendo about others be your guides. The more political a place, the better it is to be straightforward. This confuses the players, and they'll spend their time trying to figure out what you are up to. But they'll leave you alone, for the most part, because they'll think you are so clever and a brilliant player. In office politics, the votes are always being counted, but a winner is never declared.

Road Rule #57: *Sometimes it's best* not *to "be yourself."*

Your parents were probably right about you. They told you not to do this. They told you over and over and over again until you didn't even hear them. Now you do it without thinking. It's a bad habit, and heaven knows they tried to stop you from doing it your whole life. Listen. You can hear them tell you not to do it right now if you think back. "Don't talk to me in that tone of voice, young lady." "I won't have you mutter at me when you walk away. What did you say?" "Don't roll your eyes like that when I tell you something." "You are being overly dramatic about this." "Don't just stand there shuffling your feet, answer me!" Picture yourself at the dinner table, and see your parents in your mind. Imagine a finger shaking at you. Yes, now you can hear it. That thing. That thing they always claimed you did whenever they told you to clean your room. That thing you were always accused of doing when they pointed out the obvious, or told you to be in by 10 P.M. Whatever it was they told you to cut out, you'll need to cut out. Because your folks probably loved you anyway and let you keep living there despite that irritating thing you always do. Your company doesn't have to love you and they don't have to take you in again. Even at Christmas.

If a manager has to wade through what she sees as an attitude to give you an assignment or make a correction, she probably won't put on her therapist hat and think, "Why this is just a learned behavior that my employee doesn't even realize he's doing." When a manager gives you an assignment and you grimace the way you did when you were asked to mow the lawn, you'll stop getting anything good or interesting to do and start getting commands instead of opportunities. If your manager corrects you and you huff and look defensive the way you did when you were told not to leave your socks all over the house, your manager will stop correcting you and start yelling at you, just like Mom. Worse, your managers may just stop dealing with you. They'll steam quietly, and finally they'll hear one mutter too many and that will be it for you.

Road Rule #58: *They are in it for the dough.*

In even the most relaxed and creative environment, your company is paying all this rent and multiple salaries for one reason: to make money. They get most of it; you get some of it. Making money is going to be more important to your company than you getting to learn and being challenged. It is more important than you personally getting ahead. It is often more important than making sense! If you think about it, it's important to you. The same money that the capitalist pig dogs are always paying attention to translates into your paycheck, your raises, your promotions and your benefits. Because they want to make money, companies will make unpopular choices like they'll lay people off. Sometimes they'll deny you the raise you want or put limits on how much money they'll give. Often they won't hire that much-needed person, and you'll be doing far more work than seems fair. No company gives up money very easily. The ones that do don't last very long. So when you want some spent on you, make sure you've got reasons that are about the bottom line.

The kindest, warmest and most fun-loving of businesses will always be a business first and then one big happy family after. You need to remember this when you are making choices about your own career. It's important to be loyal to a point. Your company is not a person or a family. They are a business, and they can be loyal to you up to a point. So if you see layoffs ahead, get your resume out there. If you truly believe that you are being underpaid and overworked, you might want to look for another wonderful place to work that will pay you more, before you get bitter.

Road Rule #59: *Honesty is not always the best policy.*

OK, I know I said in boo-boo number 4 that honesty is the best policy. Honesty can be about what you do and say, and then there is honesty about other people. Pointing out in a meeting that the president of the company is a senile old drip may be the truth, but the truth will be of little comfort to you while you are wandering from personnel agency to personnel agency in search of a new job. Everyone else probably knows he's a senile old drip, but he's their senile old drip. There is no real need to point it out. Think of it this way: Everyone may honestly think your haircut is stupid, but pointing it out for you is a useless exercise in practicing honesty.

I do not mean to suggest that you lie. You never ever lie. But sometimes you may just want to shut up. Before you go blurting out what is painfully obvious, you might want to figure out why no one has done anything about it before. There is more going on in the boardroom and management offices than is dreamed of at your starter desk.

If you are really pushed for an opinion and your thoughts are unkind, try taking a lesson from actors, who are called upon to comment on their fellow actors' dreadful performances in some lousy plays. Some of my favorites include "You'll never know what you did" or "Only you could have done it just that way." When people are looking for compliments or confirmations, they don't need much. Just mutter something and let them hear what they like.

Be careful never to mix up the "truth" with your opinion. Of course if something illegal, like harassment or graft, is going on, you should figure out whom to talk to about it and do it. There is a fine line between honesty and the truth. Be careful not to trip over it.

Road Rule #60: *Not everyone will like you, and you won't like everyone.*

For the better part of your life you have been able to avoid or eliminate the people in your life whom you don't like. (By the way, anyone who doesn't like you has been avoiding you, too.) Now you are going to be spending five days a week with a group of people, some of whom will be distasteful to your delicate sensibilities. You don't have to like them, but you will have to work with them. Instead of openly hating anyone, it's better for you if you learn to be neutral about some people. Listen to them, answer politely and then get away from them.

Everyone at work is supposed to be an adult, and you won't be able to change anyone. If you openly hate someone and one day you find yourself in a work dispute with her, no one will hear your side of the issue. They'll know that you don't like this person and figure your problem is personal. It's better to keep those who know whom you despise to a minimum. (By the way, if you hate absolutely everyone at work, then it's probably you. You should either check your attitude, or start looking for another place where you will be happier.)

While you have been the darling in everyone's life up to this point, you will probably find that there are some people in the office who don't like you. It doesn't matter why; it will happen. Some of these people who don't like you don't matter a bit. So be nice and don't worry about it. You're charming, and it is their loss. Some of these people who don't like you will have some influence over what happens to you, and you'll want to persuade them what a fine person you are. Don't try too hard, because that usually backfires. What you can do is to focus on the work you are supposed to do and do it well. It's hard to argue with results, and results win over style almost all the time. It's better to remain neutral with the people who don't like you, win them with your business skills and let them choose to become your ally. It works.

Road Rule #61: *There is little more job security and very little loyalty.*

People get laid off. People get fired. Companies fold, get bought or restructure. Unfortunately, the business environment you are entering is not the one your folks were in. They had a good chance of staying with a company for as long as they wanted to. You don't. You can read in the papers about companies laying off as many as 40,000 people. Not all those people were moronic slackers. Some of them were working very hard and really really needed their jobs. Layoffs are now a fact of life, like ugly rock stars dating blond models and nothing in your size ever being on sale. Sure, it's possible that layoffs won't happen, but the odds get better and better that they will. It isn't pretty, it isn't nice, it sometimes isn't even right. But it happens.

So how do you develop a sense of loyalty when your company can only offer you a limited loyalty in return? Should you even try? Yes and no. What you need to develop is a sense of loyalty to your career (and a paycheck). To do this, you'll have to give some consideration to the company. It's like if you show up every day in fourth grade but don't get smarter while being there, you have to do fourth grade over and again until you get it, especially if you have to change schools. You waste a lot of your life just going over the same thing. There is lots to learn; grab at it. With every assignment you get your hands on, picture how good it's going to look on your resume.

Make sure you are giving a company what they need in order to get the training and experience you'll need to move on even if moving on means to a new company. Take advantage of any training that is offered, attend every seminar they'll let you go to, and make sure you are smarter than when you started. No company can promise you a gold watch and a nice retirement, but they can offer you a chance to learn new skills. Learn them. That way everyone wins.

Sometimes the next-to-the-worst thing happens and you survive a layoff. If you do survive, you will be feeling very sorry for yourself. This is good old-fashioned survivor guilt. Why me and not old so and so? You'll be feeling insecure.

If it didn't happen to you this time, it could happen next time. And you'll be feeling angry. How can they expect me to do my job and the job of those other people who got laid off? These feelings are all normal. When you are wallowing in self-pity, remember that this is not the worst thing that can happen in a job; it is only the second-worst thing. (By the way, this is not the time to ask for a raise so you know they love you. The layoffs were about money. The company showed they loved you by keeping you on the payroll at all.)

If you can shake off that feeling of benefiting from another's tragedy, it's a good time to try to restructure your job and pick up some new job skills. There are lots of gaps after a layoff, so go fill them. This will make you indispensable if there is a next time. Taking advantage of a layoff is a lousy way to get some cool work, but remember, your resume might be your most loyal friend for a while, so feed it all you can.

The business world is changing faster than Dennis Rodman's hair color. An industry that is strong today can be gone tomorrow, and new ones are invented every day. It is very likely that your career will be made up of assignments in a variety of companies. This means your first impression skills will need to be well-honed. You'll be starting new jobs over and over again. You are your only long-term supervisor; give yourself some reviews. Go over the skills you want to pick up next so you can add them to your toolbox. You'll need to be focused and ready to learn as much as you can as fast as you can so you can give yourself a promotion at the next assignment.

CHAPTER 8

YOUR Paycheck: The Cold, Hard Truth About Cold, Hard Cash

YOU WORK HARD, AND THEY PAY YOU FOR IT. COOL. YOU'VE PROBABLY DONE LOTS OF MATH WITH THAT promised salary and figured out that you are in the money. You may have taken that annual salary, divided it by 12 and imagined buying lattes for everyone. But wait a minute before you order doubles. All is not as it seems. Before you get your paycheck, the government is going to start nibbling away at it like a Pacman game gone mad. First, they will take out federal withholding. You may get some of this back at the end of the year, but maybe not. Then in order to be sure you have enough money for rent in the trailer park when you retire, they are going to take some for social security. Then just in case you hurt yourself ripping your hair out because there is so little left in your paycheck, disability insurance will be deducted. Maybe the state you are living in would like a little from you and maybe the county and possibly the city. Then of course there might be some deductions for your insurance. Then every little tiny penny left over is yours. Both of them.

THE BASICS

Get ready because your hardest years financially are coming up. Unless you are a member of the Mom and Dad financial assistance program, making it is tough when you're just starting out. If you are bad with your money, you will pay for it in anxiety and bad credit ratings. You aren't alone; money is a loaded issue for most people. You believe that unless you understand and manage your money well, you aren't a real grown-up. Between us, most real grown-ups don't know what they are doing either. They pay people called financial planners to understand it for them. But there is some good news: Now is the easiest time to make some smart decisions about your money and develop spending habits that could pay off big time down the road.

Road Rule #62: *Know how much it costs to be you.*

You might want to develop a budget. It will give you a picture of how much it really costs to just be you. First, take your net pay, then subtract the basics, like rent, food, electricity, water, heat, phone, car payments or public transportation, car insurance. Manicures, a five spot on the third race at Pimlico and CDs, while important, are not part of the basics list. If there is anything left over after you've taken care of the basics, that's what you can just go wild with. If there is nothing left, you can do some belt tightening. Mac and cheese was invented for first jobbers. You can write letters instead of making those long-distance calls. The great thing about writing letters is that you get to talk about yourself the whole time. You could try not to be a watt waster and run around the house wearing a sweater and turning off lights the way your dad did. Join a car pool to save on gas. Get a roommate. Find a good radio station rather than buying lots of CDs. Don't buy clothes that require dry cleaning. Whatever you do, find a way to have some money left over so you can have a life. You can be as anal retentive as you want with a budget, tracking everything, making notes and spending hours, or you can use it to let you know how much you've got to play with and then throw caution to the wind.

Road Rule #63: *Open a checking account.*

You are going to be expected to pay bills and stuff with that minuscule amount of money that actually gets to you on payday, so the first thing you should do is get a checking account. Don't just walk into the first bank you see and open an account. Most banks have the nerve to charge you to keep and earn interest on your money. Shop around; call some banks and ask them for their fee schedule. Is there a minimum balance requirement? What if you go below it? Is there a charge for withdrawals at their ATMs? How about withdrawals at other banks' ATMs? You'd be surprised how fast a $5 monthly service fee and a $1.50 ATM withdrawal fee add up to a big expense each month. Sure, you can take out more money at a time, unless you have the habit of spending up to what's in your pocket. Is the bank located someplace you can get to and back on a lunch hour? Once you've made a decision to go with one bank, it's a pain to change to a new one, so choose carefully. While you're at it, investigate a savings account. So maybe you don't have the money to put into it right now but, if you read on, you will soon. Find out now what it takes to open one and the minimum balance you have to maintain to avoid monthly fees. Again, shopping around in person or by phone will save you money in the long run.

It never seemed right to me that I could be overdrawn if there were still checks left in my checkbook. This is one of the "no one said life is fair" things that you've heard about. If you bounce a check, you'll be hit with bank charges of $10 or $15 and up. So even though the bank knows you don't have any money, they just go ahead and take what little you have to pay for handling a bounced check. A couple of bounced checks a month add up to a serious expense, not to mention a pretty bad credit report which you'll lament one day soon. This money could be better spent on reckless living. Keep track of your balance by writing it down in your checkbook and keeping receipts from ATM withdrawals. You can get checks that make carbon copies to help you remember what you've spent and where.

Road Rule #64: *Save your money. No one will do it for you.*

Once you get settled or earn that first salary increase, it's time to put some money in the bank for emergencies. If you get a raise, split the amount of the increase between you and a savings plan. Financial planners say you should have at least three to six months of living expenses available in case you need it. Of course financial planners make five times your salary, so it's easy for them to say that. But if you start by saving a little, you'll get there.

Start with direct deposit. Most employers can deposit

your paycheck directly into your bank account. There's no charge and there's no wait for the check to clear. Plus you don't have that cash in your hand to have a fight with your evil twin over whether to bank it or blow it. You can instruct the company to put a certain amount in your checking account and the rest in your savings account. So maybe start by putting $20 per check in your savings account. In some cities, that translates to just a couple of fewer beers a month, or a bus ride instead of a taxi ride. And it adds up fast. The $20 every two weeks is $40 per month, almost $500 by the end of the year. You probably won't even notice it was taken out of your check. That's the key. Learn to live without the $20 each check and just forget it's in your savings account. Then, when you want or need the money, it's there waiting for you. When you are tempted, visualize that vacation in Europe, that new car, actual furniture. If you aren't moved by happy images, visualize living in the park if you lose your job. Dip into that savings account regularly, and there's no sense in even having it.

That brings up another reason why savings accounts are such beautiful things. Interest. Some checking accounts charge you fees for taking your money and giving it back to you again. But most savings accounts offer interest payments for your deposits. Sure, it's not too much; probably only about 3 to 4 percent. But the beauty part of interest payments is that they add up over time. Its called compounding. Lets take a quick example. Deposit $100 into your savings account at 5 percent annual interest, and add $20 to that at the end of each month. At the end of the first month, you'll have $120.42. The bank gave you 42 cents as interest for keeping the money there. How thoughtful. Next month you'll have $141 and by the end of the year, you'll have saved a chunk of change. Not bad for a measly $20 bucks a month and no work.

Let's face it. Unless you are dead, at some point in your life you are going to retire. This is an eventuality that you need to prepare for. You have a couple of options. Live for the moment and then live on cat food when you are old, or start planning and saving now. After you've had a raise or two, you can start putting some money aside for the drooling years and lower your taxes at the same time.

INVESTING

The easiest way for you to prepare for that glorious day you retire is to take advantage of your company's offer of a 401(k) plan. No, this is not a very long marathon. A 401(k) allows you to contribute money right out of your paycheck before your federal taxes are deducted. Every paycheck a percentage of your gross salary will be taken out and deposited into mutual funds. The great thing about a 401(k) is you can contribute just a little bit at a time (as little as 1 percent of your paycheck). Hell, you won't even notice. Because the money is taken out before tax, the impact on your net check is less than the amount you are putting into savings. Then the money goes into a mutual fund that is managed by someone who knows far more about what's hot than you or I. Mutual Funds are where a bunch of people pool their money to get a bigger bang for the buck. You can get that great compound interest stuff going now. Some companies have plans that allow you to borrow some of the money back to buy a house or for emergency funds. Instead of paying money back with interest to a bank, you pay it back to yourself and you pay the interest to you! Companies that offer a 401(k) plan can only allow you to sign up a couple of times a year. No investment will guarantee a return on your investments, but 401(k)s have a great track record. Going to the meetings where they explain this all to you is free, so try to attend one.

401(k)s and Individual Retirement Accounts (IRAs) were designed by the government in the seventies to help people plan for their later years. The idea is for you to contribute a small amount of money each year, and the government will pretend you didn't earn that money for a while and deduct it from your taxable income. Then the interest compounds (that magic word again) free of any taxes until you retire. That's a huge savings now on your taxes and could amount to a big bundle of money by the time you're seventy.

If you don't have a company-sponsored pension plan, you can open an IRA fund at any bank, brokerage company or mutual fund. An IRA fund allows for a contribution of up to $2,000 per year, but you can contribute less. You can add money to an IRA through your company's automatic deposit, or buy it all at once. That money comes right off your taxable income; so it will help you get a tax refund from the IRS and you won't have to make tax payments on the interest. IRAs are harder to manage for some than a 401(k) because you have to be able to save the money for the minimum before they let you buy it.

Be warned, these accounts are meant to be used for retirement. If you take the money back before then, the government gets all nasty about it and taxes you and fines you and there is much unpleasantness. Use a regular savings account for vacations, special events and mini-emergencies.

A great benefit of not being able to get at a retirement account is that it can't be tapped for that great outfit or a late night ATM raid to buy one more round.

OTHER WAYS TO INVEST

OK, I'm going to talk about the stock market and bigger investing now. If you have had all you can handle for the moment, I understand completely. Thank you for your time. Now skip on ahead to the next chapter. But if you actually like thinking about money and making money from your money, read on.

Time marches on, and you've got some more money saved up from that $20 a paycheck plus interest you've been stashing. You've been taking all your dates to the early-bird specials, and though you are lonely, you've got that six-month emergency cushion in the bank. You've even taken that dream vacation and drive a car you like. What do you do with the extra money now? You're ready for the big time. Investing.

There are a few simple rules to investing. First, know the risk-reward trade-off. It is like breaking your curfew as a teenager. Some nights it was worth it, sometimes it wasn't. You measure how much fun you are having against the lecture you are going to get, and decide what to do. The more risks you are willing to take with your money, the greater your potential returns will be. If you can't bear the thought of loosing a dime, then you will likely have smaller rewards. No matter what any broker or hotshot salesperson tries to tell you, just remember: the higher the possible return, the greater the risk. Spend some time asking yourself how much you're prepared to lose to get that extra 5 percent return.

Investments can be in many forms: stocks, bonds, real estate, art, old comic books, etc. The most common investment is stocks and bonds. Stocks are shares of companies that are traded on a stock exchange. When you buy stocks, the company gets to use your money. If they make some profits, the value of the stock goes up. If they don't, well, you can guess. The goal is to sell your shares for more than you paid for them.

If you are the sort of person who can bear it, you can track how the shares of a particular company are doing every single day by looking in the business section of almost any newspaper or most on-line services. If a company had a good day (it announced higher profits or a hot new product), its stock will rise. If it had a bad day (losses were announced or a senior manager resigned), the stock will fall. The stock market is meant to be a long-term investment. Few people make the most of their money by getting on the phone daily and yelling "buy buy, sell sell," as much fun as that seems. Dividends, which a company may pay from time to time (an amount of money for each share of stock), also make owning a stock worthwhile. Over time, the single best investment you can make is in the stock market. Despite some setbacks in 1987 and the Great Depression, stocks have tended to rise over the past fifty years. If you're looking for long-term growth, there's no better place to be than the stock market. Of course, there are no guarantees and you should check with your broker first.

Bonds, on the other hand, provide a more stable source of income. These investments do not provide any ownership benefits nor do they provide unlimited return potential as do stocks. However, bonds provide a steady stream of income at a certain rate of return for a given period of time.

Here's how they work: You lend a company $1,000, and it agrees to pay you back over thirty years at an interest rate of 6 percent. You'll receive $60 each year for the next 30 years, plus your full $1,000 at the end, for a total return (in today's dollars) of $2,180.

So the secret to saving enough to be secure, and even have some big fun, is to start small—but start. Make a simple budget, and give up $10 a week for your future. If you are pale and sweaty those few days before your next paycheck, you'll want to try to manage your money so it doesn't manage you. It's such a lovely thing to be able to manage your money well enough to say "my treat" from time to time. And don't forget, you are living on the bottom of the salary scale right now. It gets better. Surviving your first job means a second and better-paying job, and then a third. But remember, it's only money.

CHAPTER 9

TIMING: The Secret to Everything

WHAT'S THE SECRET TO COMEDY? TIMING. WHAT'S THE SECRET TO RELATIONSHIPS? TIMING ONCE again. What's the secret for a hit movie, play or album? Yup. Timing may be the secret to surviving and thriving in business, too. What is all this but comedy anyway? There are two kinds of timing, the kind you can control and the kind that is totally out of your control. It is important to know the difference. While you can't control what you can't control, you can always control what you do about it.

Road Rule #65: *Timing is everything.*

Usually the kind of timing you can't control is called bad luck. Like if on your first day reporting to your new job, the job you turned down two others to take, you find that the entire place was blown away in a tornado. No one could say that's anything but bad timing. If they'd only had the courtesy to be blown away a week ago, you'd be starting your second-choice job today instead of looking for survivors. But if you spend time and energy cursing the fates, or more commonly, the management, you're wasting time. And we all know that timing is everything.

The kind of timing you can control is called good luck only by the envious. The really envious call it kissing up. The rest of us know it comes from paying careful attention, striking while the iron is hot and lying low when the iron is being hurled across the room! Good timing is as much about when not to take action as when you should make a move. And don't let yourself confuse being a strategist with a kisser-upper. You don't have to be smarmy; you have to be smart. Don't think it's kissing up to give your boss what he wants and needs. It's not kissing up at all. It's working for a living.

TIMING YOU CAN'T CONTROL	TIMING YOU CAN CONTROL
Losing business/accounts	When to ask for feedback
Company's salary and increase pools	When to ask for a raise
No openings to be promoted into	Inventing a new job
Mergers/reorganization/ change	Being a force for positive change
New management	Making a first impression again
Bad moods—other's bad moods—yours	
Workload	When and how to ask for help

WHEN AND HOW TO ASK FOR FEEDBACK

New York's Mayor Ed Koch developed a famous feedback technique simply by going around New York and asking, "How'm I doin'?" When you are the mayor of a big city, people don't mind so much when you go around annoying them like that. But in business if you don't carefully time the questions, you won't get the response you want, if you get any response at all. Don't forget, in the long run Mayor Koch lost the election. This wasn't the feedback he'd hoped for.

Road Rule #66: *You will have to ask for feedback and raises.*

All through your career, you'll need to get some sense of how other people think you are doing. If you let yourself be the only judge, depending on your ego, you'll think you are about to be fired all the time or you'll believe you are really the glue that is holding the joint together. More often than not, neither one of these things is true. To keep your imagination from running away with you, you want feedback, and lots of it.

The trouble is, most people are really lousy at giving feedback. They worry that they will freak you out if they correct you. Or they think that feedback means negative criticism and you are doing just fine, so you don't need any. Frankly, chances are they haven't been paying that much attention to you. So in order to get good feedback, you've got to learn when and how to ask for it.

When you ride a bus or subway in a new city, it's natural to ask which stop is yours over and over, just to be sure that you won't end up in some abandoned train yard at the end of the world. You aren't sure what's going on, and you need to be reassured. It's very natural to need to be reassured during a super-busy time or in the middle of a tough project. But this is not the time when your manager is going to stop everything to focus on you.

To keep your confidence up, just assume that if you were messing up big time, someone would probably make this perfectly clear to you. But if everyone is in the thick of it, this is not the time to ask someone to take their eyes off the goal or the deadline to focus on you. All they will think about your performance if you ask at the wrong time is that you tend to "get all needy" just when things get tough. When the project is over, the celebratory beers have been drunk and everyone has had a decent night's sleep is the time you should strike. You should ask for a chance to discuss how you can improve the next time. "How can I improve next time" are code words for "give me feedback."

Give the manager time to think about what she wants to say to you. If you ask for feedback on the spot, you won't get much of a response. She hasn't been keeping a running list of everything you've done and how well you've done it, so she'll need time to gather her thoughts. So schedule a time to talk with her. Say something like "Can we sit down for a couple of minutes on Friday to go over how I did on that last project? I'd really appreciate your feedback." If you play it right, the boss may even buy lunch. (That's why they call it FEEDback.)

If no one is speaking to you or looking you in the eye for a few weeks, someone is probably unhappy with you. You'd better find out what is up. Most people freeze up when they think they are getting frozen out, and it's a big

mistake. Ask to speak to your manager about your performance tomorrow. Don't put it off to spend sleepless nights
raising your blood pressure and becoming a wreck. If something is going wrong, find out what it is so you can fix it
fast. Again, give the manager time to think about what he
wants to say to you. But exercise caution, look around, see
if the manager is treating everyone the same way or if you
might just be paranoid. Also, don't ask for feedback every
day or for everything you do. If you need this constant
reassurance, call your mom. Hopefully she'll have very nice
things to say about you.

Road Rule #67: *When you ask for feedback, be
prepared to hear it.*

Be prepared to discuss how you are doing; don't expect
a speech from the boss. Often a feedback session is simply
finding out if your manager agrees with your perspective
about what kind of job you are doing. Think about what
you have done, what you've been improving and about
what you've learned from what wasn't done too well. Be
ready to talk about what you think of your performance.
Make sure you listen to what she says. This is hard, because
your inner voice will start screaming at you the moment
she mentions anything that could be improved. Don't argue,
even if you think she is wrong. Don't decide that you are
a complete failure if you haven't been perfect. What you
are hearing is her perspective, not ultimate truths. This is
about the impressions you seem to be making, not your
actual abilities or worth as a person. So remain calm if you
don't like what you hear and try to clear up any obvious
misunderstandings. If you are flabbergasted, it is OK to

say you'd like to think about all you've heard, and discuss it later.

WHEN AND HOW TO ASK FOR A RAISE

Be sure to ask for feedback first, so if you skipped that section, go back and read it now. You should ask for a raise only when you can be convincing and are convinced that your performance warrants it. You don't get a raise for being nice or for having rented an apartment you can't afford. You don't even get a raise for sitting there putting up with everyone for what seems like a very long time. This seems wildly unfair, I know. You only get a raise for doing a better job than was expected of you and adding responsibilities to the job you were hired to do. They offered you the salary you have now to do an OK job. In order to get a raise, you are going to have to talk convincingly of merit. What have you done for me lately is the song that is ringing through your boss's head when the words "salary increase" are spoken. Remember, this is money we are talking about here; their money. The cheap bastards won't give it up to you that easily!

Road Rule #68: *Ask for a raise only when you know you have earned it.*

If you are going to ask for a raise, be certain you can make your case. You need to be able to explain that you have gone above and beyond the call of duty, consistently and over time. Citing one lost weekend at your desk is like demanding to get a raise in your allowance because you actually did your chores once last year. Talk about the things you have done well every time, all that work you do so seamlessly that no one even notices it's being done anymore. Make sure that most of the extraordinary things you have been working on are completed. Again, you won't get a real evaluation right in the middle of the bedlam. While you've been busy doing the extraordinary stuff, make certain that you haven't been slacking on your regular duties. It's really easy to run around being heroic only to leave the basics undone. Doing that cool work you've been dying to do can be very time-consuming. Remember—if they didn't need someone to do those stupid things, too, they wouldn't have hired you to do them in the first place.

Don't ever ask for a raise in the days after the company has had a layoff. It's amazing how many people do this. You'll have this urge, too. You'll justify it by going over and over in your head the additional responsibilities you'll have because other people aren't there to take them on. You'll look for money as a way for the company to tell you that they like you, because all these layoffs are making you anxious. Good reasons. Bad timing. Management thinks your reward for all the extra responsibilities and the vote of confidence is that you are still on the payroll at all. Plus, you haven't proven that you can handle all the additional responsibilities yet.

At this point you can do only two things. You can tell them to stick their additional responsibilities in their ear and move in to a cheaper apartment with six or seven roommates, or you can give it three months. Do a great job, and then go in and discuss some sort of additional compensation. Three months can seem like three minutes compared to living with Vlad the psycho roomie and standing in the unemployment line for three days! If you still don't get what you think is fair, remain calm and start sending your resume out. Better to find out what's out there while you have a job than to be out there and find there is nothing there!

Don't worry if you get turned down the first time you ask for a raise. It happens all the time. If I got all the raises I deserved and asked for, I'd be rolling in it right now. If you get turned down, make sure you ask your manager what they need to see from you to be eligible for a raise next time, and when you might bring up the topic again. Give it a few months and try again. Make sure when you go back with hat in hand that you have made the kind of progress they were looking for. A couple of weeks worth of progress won't cut it.

If you do get the raise first time out, make sure you go out and buy a couple of copies of this book for your friends.

HOW TO GET PROMOTED WHEN THERE ARE NO OPENINGS

You've earned it. They are even telling you you've earned it. But you don't have it. Why? Because there is no opening for you to be promoted into. This is a dangerous time because you'll get bored with what you are doing and then want to give up. Then you'll get mad, and then you'll feel taken advantage of. Then you'll start doing crummy work to get even. Then they won't promote you when the opportunity finally appears, because you are doing crummy work.

This happens a lot. A new employee comes in like gangbusters. He is going to do everything better than anyone ever has; and he does. But three months later, he's conquered everything and wants a new job. When there is no new job, he gives up. By the time there is a promotion available, he's been such a loser that no one remembers how good he was at first. Consistency is an important component for success. Here is when you get to prove you've got it.

Often that next opportunity can be a long time in coming. You have a couple of options. One is to adopt something you may rarely have had to use before, and that is patience. Patience is not something that means you gave it a week, what more can the heartless fiends ask of you? Patience is a long-haul thing. It's like having a little brother or sister. You can't kill them, so you learn to put up with them for a long time. If you torment them, you only end up getting in trouble and they are still going to read your diaries if they can. It's sort of worth the patience.

Make sure when you are waiting out a promotion that you keep learning new stuff. We already know that's up to you. Read every fax they give you, every memo you type. Every day you are stuck doing the same old thing, you've got the chance to understand a little bit more about it.

The second way to get a promotion is more fun, and that is to be inventive. Create a new job for yourself. The first step is to figure out what they need. What isn't getting done that everyone complains about? What is barely getting done? What help could you give to that person who is going insane because she is so busy so that you could make her life easier and she'd give you the chance to do some new stuff? Don't ask permission, don't send a proposal. Just start doing it. Once you start doing it, she'll discover that she needs more of it. This is going to add more work to your life for a while.

Pretty soon, when you are the person going insane, you

can make a case that there are two jobs here and you should be promoted into the new one. Make sure the work you are doing adds value to the process. For example, they probably don't need someone to organize all the Rolodexes according to the ages of the people they are calling. The tasks you undertake should help accomplish the mission of your department or group. And make sure it's something you'd like to do and will be good at, because you'll probably end up doing it full-time. You don't want to organize Rolodexes full-time. Once you get people relying on this new and wonderful service you are providing, they won't be able to live without it. Give them a proposal now explaining that you are already doing the job and add a few new things you'd like to try. Then some other sap can do all that stupid stuff you've had to put up with. Dumping the crummy stuff on others: it's called a career.

An important reminder once again: They are paying you to do the job you have now, now matter how moronic it is, because they believe they need someone to do it. If you stop doing it well, only heartache can follow. I keep beating you over the head with this information because I've seen many an eager soul lose his job, or at least a promotion, because he stopped giving phone messages (part of his job) and invented a whole new and improved production system (not part of his job). Someone has to take the messages. It's an awful job, but someone has to do it!

HOW TO SURVIVE REORGANIZATIONS AND BAD TIMES

Bad morale. Every place has some pockets or periods of bad morale. To be honest, some places and people like bad

morale. The lousier everything is, the better. It gives everyone something to talk about and an excuse to have "just
one more beer." Bad morale can be the result of poor lead-
ership, organizational changes or just a bunch of creeps
strategically placed in the company, whose full-time jobs
seem to be making everyone miserable. Low morale happens in the best-run and most stable organizations. Sometimes it's just the weather dragging everyone's spirits down.
Bad morale can be an excuse some people use for not doing
their best, or it can be the methodical work of a couple of
disgruntled employees.

Road Rule #69: *When morale is bad, be careful
not to make it worse.*

Be very cautious: bad morale is catching. It's insidious.
It's like a romantic relationship—it's always more interesting for everyone when it's not going well. When things are
rocky in a relationship, you have lots more to talk about
and people can give you advice and sympathy. When a
relationship is going well, there is not much to say about
it. You just gaze and grin at people. Everyone finds that
dull. If you don't believe me, ride the elevator at 8:45 A.M.
in any large office building. When people ask each other
"How's it going," everyone says, without having to think
about it, "Another day another dollar," or "Thank God
it's almost Friday." They will say something derogatory like
a knee-jerk reaction. Watch what happens if someone says
"It's going great" or "I love this place." Everyone will look
at her as if she were out of her mind, and a traitor to boot.
   When morale is bad, you want to sympathize with the
victims. You hear their problems and gasp in horror. You

listen to empty plans of insurrection and cheer them on. You seem to go out for beers after work more often and bond. It doesn't take long before you, too, will want to rally around a common enemy. You begin to mutter "heartless worm" under your breath when a supervisor walks by. You start to gather evidence that your friend or friends are right. Pretty soon you are just as miserable as everyone else. And that makes everyone happy.

It's natural and advisable to understand your coworkers' points of view, but make sure your miseries are your own. When you do have a misery, fix it, don't wallow in it (no matter how marvelous that feels). "Take this job and shove it" may be a fine country-western song and an exhilarating fantasy, but it don't pay the rent. It's very easy to have your own experiences in a company feel less real than everyone else's. For example, you are having a perfectly lovely morning and then you go to lunch with someone who is the soul of crankiness. Suddenly nothing seems so sunny. You spend the rest of the day hating everyone and everything, too. Listen to your own drummer, especially when everyone is cranking. Own your life, damn it! You deserve it.

Whenever a company goes through a change, morale gets bad. You can count on it. If there is a merger, there is bad morale. If there are management changes or layoffs, there will be bad morale. People begin to worry about their jobs and who the hell all these new people are. When there is a reorganization, bad morale is brewing because someone new may be in charge and someone else has been deposed, and people from the old regime are burned up about it, so they get busy telling everyone what a stupid mistake was made. If there are layoffs there will be bad morale because all the survivors feel insecure, and have survivor guilt. These are all normal feelings and not unfounded. Go ahead and have them. Feel crummy, mutter about how dumb management is or how awful the new owners are. But don't stay in that gray space too long. Because if you linger too long, you'll find yourself trapped by your own bad morale.

You'll need to do something about it eventually (or wait to get fired, because that's where you are headed). Sooner or later you'll need to look for a new job, learn how to do your job in a new way or meet the new management and find out for yourself what they are really like.

Most things that bring about bad morale have one thing in common: change. Suddenly what you do, whom you do it for or where you do it is different. You have to prove yourself all over again. Or you start to worry that you won't be able to do it a new way or please the new bosses. This kind of low morale is really about not wanting to go through change and learn all the new things you have to learn. Change is always scary and always hard. And change always happens no matter how hard you try to sit still. It is one of those love-hate things. People love change that they control, like getting a promotion, or moving to a new place. They hate change they can't control, like someone else getting the promotion or moving to a new place.

Pardon my sweetness-and-light attitude, but it's true that all change has opportunities in it. It just takes a little longer to find them when you don't choose the change for yourself. You know how your dad can't program the VCR? This is how it starts—looking at change like something mysterious that you can't manage or understand. If you don't find a way to see change as an opportunity for yourself (like watching any TV show you want any time you want) and learn how to make it work for you, you're in danger of becoming your old man! Now that is a terrifying change.

WHEN AND HOW TO MAKE A FIRST IMPRESSION ALL OVER AGAIN

Sooner or later that saint or creep you are working for will be replaced by another saint or creep. Eventually your manager will be promoted, transfer, quit or be fired. Or you will be promoted, or transferred. Then you have to start all that kissing-up stuff all over again. Those handy phrases you were comfortable with in Turkey won't be useful when you get to Greece. You need to figure out where you are and use a new phrase book.

Road Rule #70: *Be prepared to forget everything and learn it again.*

This is an easy place to trip up. Having proved yourself to your last manager doesn't mean a thing. You have to start that first-impression process all over again. Don't take this personally. Everyone has to do it. Your new boss has to do it, too! In fact, this is something you'll have to do over and over again before anyone gives you a watch and sends you off to a home. So you'll be better off if you learn to do it well.

When you start a new job at a new company, everyone and everything are different. So naturally you understand that you'd better show off the best parts of you and comb your hair every day. But when you change positions or departments in your current company, your guard is down because everything else is familiar. Those things that you didn't have to show off anymore because everyone knew you were good at, well, no one knows now. At best your boss is trusting the positive rumors about you, but he's waiting for you prove your brilliance to him. The simple things that you were trusted to do once, no one trusts you to do now. You've got to prove everything all over again.

Try to think of it as dating. You may go to the same restaurant that you used to frequent with your ex; but the first time you take someone new there, you probably shouldn't get all comfortable and chew with your mouth open and belch after a satisfying sip of soda. (At least I hope you don't. If you do, then this may explain the number of lonely evenings you spend reading self-help books.)

You need to prove all over again how smart you are, your willingness to do whatever it takes and your trustworthiness. And you better do it right away, or you'll be starting from behind. Best behavior is called for. In addition there will be things your last boss didn't care about that this one does, and there will be things you may have killed yourself doing that don't matter at all now. Every manager you have will have his own style and his own sense of what's important. Once again, you can't expect anyone to stop everything and lay it all out for you. So ask questions and make sure you let the manager know what you are doing and how you do it. Ask him what his mission is for the department. Ask how his team works together. Be prepared to forget everything you know and learn it all again.

WHEN AND HOW TO SURVIVE BAD MOODS

Everyone is entitled once in a while. The blues, the cranks, existential angst, rage, general poopiness. You know you have the right, and by golly you will exercise that right. However, you might not realize that everyone you work with is also entitled to be a big drip from time to time, too. If you don't know this, you are going to get mad when it happens or get your feelings hurt. If you don't pay attention to it, your timing will be disastrous.

YOUR BAD MOODS

Life keeps happening to us, even when it is inconvenient. So go ahead and be in a bad mood. Enjoy. But the trick is to not take it out on anyone else. Hide in your office. Put on a phony smile and think hateful things about everyone. Type curses onto your computer as fast as you can. Don't print that, though; don't even save it. Put a time limit on your wallow. Most people will allow you to be a pathetic slob or a tightly wound crank for a few days, but don't let yourself go longer than a week. If you are going to weep every time someone asks you if you've picked up that package from the mail room, people will be willing to work around you for a while, but ultimately they'll have to find someone to replace you. When you look as if you are going to reach for a handgun when you are asked if that memo went out, people will avoid you. While being avoided may bring the peace you are looking for, if it keeps up, soon you'll find yourself alone with daytime talk shows instead of with coworkers.

Road Rule #71: *It is professional to take good care of yourself.*

If you feel a good misery episode coming over you, try to save it up for the weekend. Pick up some weepy music and Oreos on your way home and go to it. But don't let this miserable person become the permanent you. If you have to take a couple of days off to get over it, then try to do that. If you can't get out of it, get some help. Lots of companies have employee-assistance programs, with therapists that fall within the insurance guidelines. You can't afford not to take good care of yourself.

THEIR BAD MOODS

First, don't take it personally. The last thing anyone who's just cranky wants is for you to be needy all over her. All it will do is give her a place to focus her anger—on you! If it goes on, follow the one-week rule you've given yourself. Then go tell her you've noticed that she hasn't been herself lately and you want to make sure it's not anything you've done. If she says no, believe her. Ask if there is anything you can do. Then let it go. Second, don't get mad. If the person isn't usually like this, try not to pick a fight. Be a better person than she is, and then you can be smug about it with your friends. If you get mad at her, you are only going to escalate everything, often beyond repair.

When either one of you is in a bad mood, it is not the best time to ask for anything special. When you are in a bad mood, you don't want to be very accommodating, and she doesn't either. It is worth waiting to ask for the raise, promotion, feedback or time off until you can get what you want. If you really can't wait (and I beg you to try), then a good strategy begins with figuring out the source of her foul mood and making your request as far away from that source as possible. If you think her personal life is in the toilet, wait until the end of the day. That way she's had a full day of work between her and the horrors of her home life, or lack of it. If you believe that work is the source, then get to her early in the morning, before she's run the gauntlet. And make sure she knows that she won't be inconvenienced in any way by your request. A little timing goes a long way toward getting what you want when you are stuck dealing with humans and all that goes along with them.

HOW TO SURVIVE A CRAZY WORKLOAD AND WHEN TO ASK FOR HELP

No one actually means to kill you with too much work, but frankly, they probably aren't thinking too much about it one way or the other. The work has to get done, the customer served, the deadline met, and that's all anyone is thinking about. Most businesses have a heavy season, but they staff for the lean times. That means sooner or later everyone has a workload that feels like they're being asked to single-handedly build a pharaoh's pyramid by 5 P.M. Impossible? Yes, but they want it done anyway.

Road Rule #72: *You'll have too much to do sometimes.*

When your "in" box is taller than you are, it's time to panic, prioritize and produce. Yes, panic. Go ahead and get it over with. It will get your adrenaline up. You need the energy. Try not to go screaming down the halls or anything. But saying "Oh God, oh God, OH GOD" a few times in a private place will do you a world of good. If you don't let yourself panic for a minute, then you freeze. When you are on overload you might frequently wake up in the middle of the night in a panic. Go ahead and panic for a while, then do something about it, because sleep is so great. Since you can't usually fix anything in the middle of the night, you should prioritize. Make a quick game plan. First things first. What should you do second? What can you pass off . . . uh, I mean delegate to someone else? Write it down, and then call your office voice mail and read the list yourself. Now you don't have stay up worried about forgetting to bring your list in the morning. Then it's sweet dreams for you.

Set your priorities, and then check them with someone. No use spending half a day getting shipping labels ready only to find that Morris in the mail room already did it. What you might think belongs toward the bottom of the list may be the thing that brings the dogs baying at your office door in an hour. So make sure your list makes sense to someone else, too. Also, you want to make sure your manager sees how much you've got going on (this comes in handy later if you have to ask for help).

Now you've got to produce. Get some results. Once you get one thing off that list, you are going to feel a whole lot better. The old journey-of-a-thousand-miles thing. It only takes one step to make a start. If you don't get that first thing off the list, you'll go right back to panic. Then the whole episode gets dragged out and you lose more lovely sleep. More important, if your manager sees lots of smoke from you but no fire, you won't be able to get the help you need later. If he sees you are accomplishing as much as you can, you win points.

But how long do you let this insanity go on? A busy patch is one thing, but having gray hair and a nervous tick at the age of twenty-four is too much. Before they find you whimpering under your desk, you might want to ask for help. If you are going to ask someone else for help, there are a couple of things you need to ask yourself first. Is everyone else working at this pace? If they are, this might be what's expected. How long has this been going on around here? If it's a psycho period, you'd be better off to just buck up and get through it and plan a long vacation when it's over. Are you ever actually knocking things off your list? If not, you are running around in circles a lot, and they won't pay two people to make up for inefficiencies. They'll pay just one person who doesn't happen to be you. Give up a weekend day or a couple of evenings in the office to get ahead of yourself, and see if you don't feel better.

Road Rule #73: *Managers don't read minds.*

If you do believe that getting help is in order, bring the ammo with you when you go to ask for reinforcements. Have a detailed list of what you are working on and how long it will take to complete each item. You might find you have things on your list that no one cares about but you. Getting these projects killed may keep you from killing yourself. Be ready to discuss the benefits that the company gets by dividing the job. Or is there someone else in the group who could do some of your stuff more efficiently?

Make sure you are willing to sacrifice doing some cool stuff. Managers see right through it when all you want to get rid of is the dull stuff. You could even suggest that a part-time person or a temp be hired to get you to the end of your long march. Be sure of yourself before you ask because there was probably only one person who did your job before you got there and she did all right. Or did you see her name in the obituaries?

> **Road Rule #74:** *Be extra nice to yourself when*
> *work isn't nice to you.*

If you don't get help (and this is very likely in this economy), don't spend time thinking that they hate you. Instead, innovate yourself out of this pickle. Who are untapped resources that you could get involved to give you some room? Great secret sources are the receptionist and that bright young kid in the mail room. Usually these people are dying for something interesting to do. When there is no help available, streamline whatever you can. Don't rush anything. When you rush, you make more mistakes and have to do things twice. You don't have time for that. Dig into your psyche to find that anal-retentive you, and put her in charge.

Make sure you use your personal time well. Take bubble baths, rent movies, sleep a lot, take drives, treat yourself to a new CD instead of benders. Often when we stress or are overworked the only person who isn't taken care of is you. Be nice to yourself. Remember that eventually you'll retire. Then you can mutter about these lazy kids nowadays. Why, when you were starting out . . .

WORK SHEET # 4

The Good Timing Work Sheet

You want something: a raise, a promotion, feedback, a week off, help, something. Well, everyone wants something. I'm afraid you are going to have to ask for what you want. Squeaky wheels get the grease. But if there is no grease around, the squeaky wheel will just be irritating. Before you ride into battle, best to scope out the territory. And have a battle plan; i.e., make sure there is grease and that someone has a reason to give it to you.

Take the test below, and make sure you have a score of 25 or more before you make the move. If your score is 40, proceed with obnoxious confidence!

_____POINTS
This morning my boss:

- *Got yelled at by his boss (0)*
- *Came in whistling a happy tune (3)*
- *Has a hangover (1)*
- *Finished a big project and I helped (4)*

The last thing my boss said last night was:

- *Another day, another dollar (3)*
- *I expect to see that memo corrected by 9 A.M. (0)*
- *I understand they fired the whole sales department today (0)*
- *Thanks for everything (You may only think you heard this; it may have been a hallucination. Score carefully.) (5)*

The last three tasks I completed:

- *Completed? You mean I was supposed to finish them? (0)*
- *Were late and had mistakes in them (0)*
- *My boss said, "What? Done already?" (5)*
- *Went completely without notice (3)*

I've had this job:

- *Since last Tuesday (1)*
- *Longer than anyone else has been able to stand it (3)*
- *No less than six months (3)*
- *Because I'm being cursed by God (1)*

The company as a whole is:

- *Fiscally sound (3)*
- *Going to be featured on 60 Minutes this Sunday (1)*
- *Just won some new accounts (4)*
- *Cutting in every department (0)*

When I get the chance to ask for what I want

- *I am able to explain it, defend it and have examples ready (4)*
- *I'll probably cry, because I'm so upset (1)*
- *I can be specific (one sentence can explain it) (3)*
- *I'm going to give that lousy bastard a piece of my mind (0)*

If I don't get what I want I'll:

- *Make sure I understand why, so I can get it next time (4)*
- *Send those photographs from the Christmas parties to senior management (1)*
- *Reformulate my arguments and try again later (2)*
- *Hold my breath till I get what I want (0)*

CHAPTER 10

REVIEWS: How Can They Say Those Mean Things About Me?

IMAGINE GOING UP TO SOMEONE IN YOUR PERSONAL LIFE AND ASKING HIM TO WRITE DOWN AND DISCUSS ALL THE things that he likes and dislikes about you. Think about what your family might say in a short paragraph about your performance as a member of the family. Imagine what your best friends would say if they were to list your strengths and weaknesses. What would your girlfriend or boyfriend say about you if she or he had to rate your skill as a date on a scale of one to five? Scary, huh? Now imagine how angst-ridden you might be if the person who holds the key to your continued employment and ability to buy groceries were to sit down and list your strengths and weaknesses, evaluate your skills and discuss what you need to improve. It is called a review. And you are going to get one.

Road Rule #75: *Managers don't like to do reviews.*

Reviews are designed to give you formal feedback. They are the vehicle for praising you and, much to your chagrin, letting you know what you need to do better. Most companies conduct reviews at least once a year, and many companies do them even more often. This is the one time your manager sits down and actually thinks about how you are doing. In fact, this may be the first time your manager has even thought about what he wants you to do, let alone how well you are doing it. So don't be surprised if there are surprises on your first review.

There are as many reviewing styles as there are managers. Some will just grunt and hand you a piece of paper with rating numbers circled. This will not be very satisfying; it's like getting up the nerve to ask someone if he loves you and he replies, "Well, you're, um, well, OK I guess." See if you can coax a little more info from the reviewer if you get this kind of review. Try asking, "Have you thought about having me beaten to a pulp?" or "Possibly you'd like to adopt me?" This is no time to be shy.

Other managers will write out long, well-crafted paragraphs that don't tell you anything. You'll be tempted to approach this like poetry and find the deep meanings, but you'll probably be wrong. Some people just aren't very clear in their own minds about what's working and what isn't. If you want the feedback you need, read the review a couple of times and try to calmly ask questions that get yes or no responses.

Road Rule #76: *A good review will tell you the bad and the good.*

I'm sorry to have to tell you this, but if you get a glowing review without a whisper about what you could possibly do better, you may have been ripped off. Sure, you should bask in the glow, even celebrate; but don't forget, nobody's perfect. It's a good bet your manager didn't take the time to really think about what you could do better, or possibly she is a pathological liar. Maybe he doesn't know how to tell you what he needs. If your review is perfect, make sure to ask for new goals. Managers like that. It tells them you want to keep growing, and it's a way for them to tell you what you could do better without the risk of your flipping out and leaving in a huff. And it gives you something new to shoot for. It's even possible that you may be doing a perfect job. Now that you have achieved perfection, if you don't set new goals with your manager, you will be lofty and bored in no time.

If your review is chock-full of "needs improvements," don't panic. Try not to cry and try not to call anyone names. If you panic, you won't be able to hear what they are telling you. Criticism isn't designed to destroy your self-esteem but to let you know what isn't working so that you can fix it. And don't get defensive, for heaven's sake—even if you think your manager is out of his mind and not paying attention to the million things you do right.

One of two things usually happens when a review is on the "tough" side. Either the reviewed one thinks that the manager is a hateful bastard, who is clearly and methodically out to get her. Or the reviewed one believes he is totally worthless, and it's hopeless, and everyone in the company is talking about what a loser he is, and why even try because he is such an abysmal failure anyway. Surprisingly, neither of these lines of thinking will be of much use to you. Nor will they ever be true.

If you get corrected or even slammed in a review, don't forget that for some reason, your manager believes these things about you. There is no reason for him to make up crummy stuff to say about you. You might think his opinion of your performance is wrong. Or you might think he is right, BUT it's not your fault. It doesn't matter. All that matters is that your boss believes it. So don't argue about it. You've just been given the scoop about what's bugging him. If the only thing really wrong is his perceptions about your work, well, that's nothing. You can fix that. If he thinks you miss deadlines, but you know it's really the fault of that idiot in finance who didn't get you the numbers, all you have to do next time is tell your manager where you are having trouble before the deadline hits. If your manager doesn't think you do enough, but you think you are a machine, drop little statements every day or so about what you've accomplished today. If he doesn't think you know how to prioritize, don't rush headlong into a project without discussing what's on your plate and what he'd like to see first. See? When you understand that a criticism is just someone's perception, you can change the view.

Road Rule #77: *Don't air your bad review all over the company.*

It's never a good idea to go complaining all over the place about what a raw deal you got. Your friends at work will all agree that your review was completely unfair and wrong. They will back you up on every complaint. That's why they are called friends. Your coworkers' opinions, while comforting, won't help you get a raise or even keep your job. Worse, their indignation on your behalf will probably add fuel to your fire. Pretty soon, you'll not only be a poor performer in your manager's eyes, you'll also have a "bad attitude."

Blow off steam about a bad review with your friends who aren't in the office. They can agree with you over every beer, but you'll never be accused of having a bad attitude at work. Instead of gathering evidence from coworkers about how wronged you have been, quietly devise a plan for being so great that "you'll show the egomaniacal moron." Then ask the reviewer if you can meet and discuss your progress in thirty days.

Most of your reviews will be somewhere between a nomination for sainthood and a condemnation to hell. Make sure that you don't see just one side of the review. Most of us hear one bad thing about ourselves, and it's like the starting gun going off in the self-obsession marathon. While there are gray or neutral areas in most reviews, most employees' reactions are either black or white. Don't let 'em mess with your mind and don't mess with it yourself.

There are things you can do to prevent a bad review. When you first start your job, find out from personnel what the review policy is. It's a good idea to ask for a blank review form. Study it. It will tell you all the criteria that you will be judged on when review time comes around. How often in your life are you going to get a crib sheet to work from? Take advantage. This review form will tell you what the company thinks is valuable in an employee. Is there lots of emphasis on working well with others? Then you'd better slop on the charm. Is the review mostly about achieving goals? Then you might want to sit down with your boss as soon as possible and set some goals for yourself and find out what the team goals are.

Road Rule #78: *They are watching you every day.*

It's not your fault, really it isn't. You learned it in school. Since you were six years old, you have been taught that you can slack off, do as little as possible. Then if you hustle a little you make up for it on the test. By the time you bring your report card home all that undone homework is forgotten. College is designed so that you can be a big mess for three months, then do a little cramming and still pass the final. Managers have memories like elephants. Don't be surprised if you have to relive all your mistakes in your review. Every day is a pop quiz.

Road Rule #79: *You still have time to improve.*

When you sit down for your first review, if it's not all you hoped it would be, you may be wondering why no one ever told you when the midterms were. No midterms or finals where you could redeem yourself, and suddenly they are giving you a report card. When you read the review, you find that the deadline you missed and tried to blame on everyone else in the Western world was really a pop quiz, and those four Fridays in a row when you called in sick must have been the final. Listen for the clues every day. You can tell if something is getting under someone's skin. If you mess up and someone says, "Yeah, well, OK I guess," that means "I will remember this, and you'd better not make the same kind of mistake again." If you think this episode is over, you are wrong. What long and unforgiving memories these guys have. Geez.

All of us want feedback. We want to know how we are doing. Are we loved? Do we make a difference? Trouble is, in a review, they actually tell us.

W O R K   S H E E T   # 5

Review Thyself: Typical Review Questions

Below are some typical questions your manager will ask herself about you come review time. Read them over and review yourself. Think of your performance compared with all the other people in your department. Would you give yourself a raise? Would you recommend yourself for a promotion?

List the employee's strengths:

    1.
    2.
    3.

List the employee's weaknesses:

    1.
    2.
    3.

What was the employee's major accomplishment this year?

On a scale of one to five, five being excellent, how would you rate the employee in the following areas:

SKILL	Poor				Excellent
Communication skills	1	2	3	4	5
Timeliness of work delivery	1	2	3	4	5
Responsible	1	2	3	4	5
Attention to detail	1	2	3	4	5
Presentation skills	1	2	3	4	5
Ability to get along with others	1	2	3	4	5
Initiative	1	2	3	4	5
General understanding of job	1	2	3	4	5
General understanding of company	1	2	3	4	5
General understanding of procedures	1	2	3	4	5
Attendance	1	2	3	4	5
Knowledge of equipment and computer programs	1	2	3	4	5

In order to be ready for a promotion, what skills must the employee acquire?

What are the employee's goals for the next six months?

What should the employee be doing a year from now?

How will I as a manager help the employee?

CHAPTER 11

All Those Other People

IT MAY BE A SMALL WORLD, AFTER ALL, BUT THEY SURE HAVE PACKED A WHOLE LOT OF PEOPLE INTO IT. IF YOU wander through the crowds on Fifth Avenue in New York City at lunchtime, you'll bump into a good percentage of them. Some of them will say excuse me as they push past you, most won't. Some of the people you think are rude are just in a hurry; some of the people who say excuse me will be picking your pocket. Some will be elegant and refined, some crude and disturbed. They are all there. As you travel around there will be as many kinds of people as you can imagine. If you think everyone is mean and out to get you, that's what you'll find. If you think almost everyone is exotic, that's what you'll find. The truth is, there is a little bit of everybody in the world. Believing in the best and knowing there is the worst is probably a smart way to travel.

YOUR COWORKERS

You've learned to suck up to your boss without leaving your lips in a permanent pucker position. Now that you've mastered that, you'll want to figure out how to handle that crowd that someone has mistakenly named "your peers." To call all these different people peers is one of the misnomers of the century. Your coworkers are going to be as diverse, as strange, as smart, as goofy, lazy, tricky, brilliant and different from you as any glump of people packed into a cubicle could be. Since you are going to be hanging around with these peers of yours more than anyone else, it's best to get a handle on them.

If only all your coworkers were as dedicated, clear thinking, clever and loyal as you. It's to be wished, but never attained. If you can't manage these folks, they can manage you right out of a job.

There are three kinds of people in the office—one group who hates everything, one group who doesn't notice anything at all and one group who loves everything. Now, I actually think it's a little more complicated than that. I believe that if I walked around any office and handed everyone a hundred dollar bill, there would be people who would take credit for having thought of it, people who would tell everyone that the money came from a slush fund, some who would be angry that we are giving everyone a hundred dollars when we didn't give poor Joe a raise, some who would wonder why we gave money to that loser, Joe, and people who would be upset that we didn't get a signed receipt from everyone. Some folks would even be delighted that we gave them a hundred bucks. I think it's a happier experience if you aim at delighting folks even when you know some folks refuse to be delighted.

> **Road Rule #80:** *You won't like everyone and everyone won't like you.*

These are the people you work with. Better figure out how best to live with, enjoy and thrive among all these coworkers. It isn't easy, I'll say that. Just when you have figured out how to deal with everyone in the universe, someone you hadn't even imagined shows up and ruins your genius. Humanity, what a pain.

If you are really honest with yourself or paranoid, some of the people you read about in this chapter will be you. That's a creepy thought. When you find yourself the recipient of some of the following strategies, go home and give yourself a good talking to.

THE PLAGIARIST: GREAT IDEA! GLAD I THOUGHT OF IT

You are sitting in a big meeting ready to talk about how to improve communications in your group. You've been thinking about it and have lots of great ideas that are going to make you look smart as hell. You've got notes in hand and are practicing your speech in your head. "Short weekly meetings to keep everyone informed. Smart thinking! E-mail that requires more than one reply should immediately become an old-fashioned conversation. Brilliant! All e-mail about customer issues should be saved in the file server so that they can be referred to. Sheer genius!" Your stuff is going to make a difference. You care, you've worked on this, you know it's going to show!

You come out of your daydream about sitting in a big corner office to hear one of your coworkers marveling on about the efficient use of e-mail, weekly meetings, and a central memo file. "That's smart thinking" you say to yourself. "I couldn't agree more." "That's brilliant, that's sheer genius." "That's MY idea!" Then you remember talking to this person about your great thinking. You realize she has stolen your ideas. You stammer. You point stupidly to your notes, but it's too late. Your coworker is going to be the golden child and you are going to go in the stairwell and cry. Horrifying? It happens.

THE BAD NEWS

I really hate to break it to you, but there really are people that will take credit for your ideas. Some of these people are poor misguided slobs, just trying to get along like you. Some are evil incarnate.

I have a friend who had a report she was working on taken from her desk while she was on vacation. The report was presented while my friend sat innocently on the beach. She came back to find that her coworker had been promoted and her ideas implemented.

Given the thousands of people you'll work with in your career, chances are you'll run into a morally bankrupt idea-less poop who will try to build his career on other people's work. He will listen carefully to your ideas, encourage you and casually walk into the big cheese's office and kick around "something that's been on my mind." Are you going to let this go on? I think not.

WHAT YOU CAN DO

It probably isn't advisable to leap up in the meeting and scream, "Rat Fink Creep." This lacks that smooth professional demeanor that you've been trying so hard to cultivate. You don't want to follow this person around for the rest of the day crying "But I thought of that! You know I thought of that!" Both of these tactics will get you in a small room with personnel kindly suggesting that you take a break.

Road Rule #81: *Don't get even; get professional.*

There are several approaches you can take here; it just depends on what you can pull off. Be sure that this isn't just a strange coincidence before you do anything. One thing about most brilliant ideas is that they are usually just common sense. That means that more than one person may have thought of them. If you are really sure that you have been robbed of your intellectual superiority, then go ahead and do something about it.

You can interrupt the idea thief as he babbles on during the meeting and say, "Yes, when I was discussing this with Toadbrain here, I said . . ." Then take over the discussion. I must warn you, this requires being prepared. You can rarely pull it off because you'll be so flabbergasted the first time it happens that you'll use all your energy to keep yourself from muttering "Duh duh duh." So save this one for the next meeting you attend with the thieving dog.

You could steal one of his ideas and present it. I wouldn't recommend this. If he had any good ideas of his own he'd have used them, so you may end up presenting a lemon.

Or if the idea is any good, it's probably been plagiarized, and two wrongs . . .

Labeling and naming all your notes is a cover-your-behind method that is only worth the time if you are prepared to do something about it. There is no point in taking all that time if all you are going to do is look at it and be bitter. If you have proof that the idea is yours, take a breath, even sleep on it. Then calmly go rat out the fink to your supervisor. Let her know for informational purposes only. Don't ask that the plagiarist be tarred and feathered. Just let it sink in where it counts, and move on.

You can corner this person after the meeting and say, "Great idea, how ever did you think of it?" Then give a shriveling look and walk meaningfully toward the president's office. This may frighten the person to not mess with you again. If you don't have a shriveling look, start practicing in the mirror now.

The best bet is to mention your great idea just prior to the meeting to a couple of other folks. If it happens again, tell two or three of your friends, and mention it to your supervisor. Then let it go. If it happens again, start looking up books on Karma, even leaving one on the offender's desk.

Be careful you don't go overboard and hold every thought and idea close to the vest, speaking to no one and trusting no one. Being a good team worker is important, and you can't do that if you spend your career covering your behind. (For more information about this see the section on Anal Retentive). You can triple-lock all your doors, buy an expensive encryption device for your computer, and put a small video camera in the corner of your office. When people ask how you are, you say, "I would tell you, but then I'd have to kill you." Since this is your first job, it's a long time to go without having any friends. When you wear a trench coat and dark glasses into the office, trust me, you've gone too far.

THE GOOD NEWS

Clearly you are a smart-thinking, brilliant genius, or they wouldn't be stealing your ideas. Remember there will be lots of meetings, lots of reports and lots of opportunities to show off. The truth will come out; it always does.

OK, so on occasion some rat does steal other people's work. It doesn't happen so much that you should live your work life like a CIA operative. It's just wise to learn your lesson when this happens to you and never confide in that person again.

THE OFFICE GOSSIP: LET ME WHISPER IN YOUR EAR

Just what is management thinking? Who's going to be fired, promoted or transferred? Who is dating whom? What's the real story on the mail room person's sudden and unexplained vacation? The office gossip knows. The office gossip tells. The office gossip tells stuff he doesn't even know. He knows about people he's never even seen. He knows all, he tells all. Gossips are some of the most compelling people in the workplace. They are no good for you.

Every office has one or more world-class gossips. Sometimes gossip is the principal production of a company. It is all anyone works on or thinks about. Unfortunately gossip is a product that no one but the people who work in a given company are going to pay for. Believe me, you pay for it.

Road Rule #82: *Office gossip is fascinating and dangerous to play.*

The office gossip is going to be able to share every detail of everyone's life. This is fascinating. Nothing is more interesting than everyone else's life or anything that is none of your business. That's why we watch TV and read books. You can spend thousands of hours with the office gossip. She will horrify you, amuse you, shock you. It's grand. Whenever you get five minutes alone, you know that Radio Station T.R.A.S.H. will be on the air and broadcasting.

THE BAD NEWS

Did you ever stop to wonder how the gossip gets a lot of the really juicy stuff? Why, from talking to friends of course. Friends like you. Friends who hear a little something from him, confide a little something to him, hear a little more, tell a little more. Don't think for one second that every word you are telling your pal isn't being shared with anyone who will huddle close enough to hear the whispers about your wild life. Gossip is so compelling because there is often an element of truth in it. But it's only an element. The part about others' motivations or thoughts is pure conjecture. You never know why anyone does anything.

WHAT YOU CAN DO

When you are cornered by the office gossip (this is how she approaches) you can be polite, look away as if you are having a great thought and change the subject. You must never ever tell this person anything about yourself, about what you think, who you like or dislike. Talking to this person is like posting your personal experiences on the public e-mail. Not wise. When you stop supplying information, the gossip will leave you alone like the dried-up source you are. When you stop gasping with shock—"No! you're kidding"—the gossip will start spilling it to someone less wise and professional. If you don't manage your time with your big-mouthed pal you can be sure people will be talking about you. They'll all believe you are a gossip, too.

Whatever you do, don't get a reputation for being a gossip. People with any discretion will avoid you. Your managers won't trust you, so they will steer clear of the kind of conversations where mentors are made. Your coworkers know that talking to you may be cheaper than renting a billboard, but no less effective. This is not a compliment.

The hardest case you'll ever encounter may lead to drastic measures. Be direct with the person. Finally after hearing something very private about a friend of yours you might say, "You know, this latest tidbit is very private and I'm uncomfortable talking about it. I'd appreciate it if you wouldn't talk to me about stuff like this anymore." Believe me, they stop. The direct approach usually shames the worst gossip into leaving you out of it. Out of it is where you really want to be.

THE GOOD NEWS

Hanging out with the office gossip will give you the opportunity to laugh uproariously behind all your coworkers' backs. Of course, everyone will know this and never want to speak to you. They'll figure you're telling every little thing, too. Also, hanging out with the office gossip lets you be upset about things going on in the company long before they actually happen, if they ever do. So you'll be using Tums before your time.

Gossip is so compelling because there is often an element of truth to it. But it's only an element. The part about others' motivations or thoughts is pure conjecture. You never know why anyone does anything. And never forget, it might be your life racing along the grapevine any time soon. Do unto others . . . that's what they say.

THE HARBINGER OF DOOM:
MISSION IMPOSSIBLE

Some folks are drawn to doom like a chocaholic to Godiva. A lightbulb goes out, and this signals that the whole place is falling apart and soon you'll be working in complete darkness. The company has an office picnic so that everyone will just be hung over and one day behind in their work. Someone leaves the company, and it's a sign that the rats are leaving the sinking ship. You are dealing with a harbinger of doom. If you hang out here, you'll soon see the world just as they do: as a slow, painful root canal.

Road Rule #83: *Cynicism is only an excuse not to move.*

Sometimes harbingers are cynical. This means that they hate everything, but they are clever talking about it. They sound really smart. They are wry and funny as they convince you that everything sucks and there is no point in doing anything about it. You feel so hip while you talk about how misguided management is, and what idiots everyone else is. You never discuss how to fix anything, at least not with anyone who could do anything about it, because that would be uncool. Any ideas anyone else offers about making things better are really naive. All signs of hope are laughable. This saves everyone the effort of trying. They smirk and shake their heads knowing how fruitless it is to try.

Cynics are very dangerous people to an organization and to you, too. Not only do they believe everything stinks, they will also make you feel foolish if you don't agree. When you are with a cynic you either believe everyone else is an idiot or the cynic thinks you are the idiot.

Sometimes the harbinger simply walks around moaning about everything. She makes you feel sorry for her, you wonder why management and everyone else is so cruel to her. Unhappiness is the only thing to talk about, so you look for things in your life so you can stay in the conversation. If an assignment comes to your team, you can both look down toward hell and shake your heads. Another day, another living nightmare. At least you have someone to share it with.

THE BAD NEWS

Rotten stuff happens at work. People don't get the promotions they want, sometimes fairly and sometimes unfairly. People quit, get fired or laid off. There are reorganizations, lost customers, missed deadlines and nincompoops. There. I've said it.

You will have coworkers who focus on every horrid event and cultivate it until it grows so it's all they can see and talk about. Bad news is fuel for cranky people. When you hang out with these folks, soon that is all you'll see too. You'll either be close to tears or in a depressive exhaustion all the time. This isn't good for you physically, mentally or professionally.

WHAT YOU CAN DO

First be sure when someone tells you over and over that everything sucks big green eggs, that you get away from this person for a while and figure out what your own experiences are. Some things do suck; some things don't. If you have trouble understanding what *you* know to be awful from what others know to be awful, avoid these people at all cost. The ability to know what is your life and what is others' is a principle of mental health. If you are going to believe someone else's perception of the world, go hang out with some cockeyed optimists. At least that way you'll be happy.

Road Rule #84: *You have the power to raise your happiness level above the misery level.*

The miserable will be right about some things: some stuff really does stink. But I assure you that everything doesn't. Figure out what you can do about the stinky parts, whom you can talk to about it, and then do it. Learn to take action about what's going wrong. Understand you can't always fix it, but it's worth a try.

Now comes the fun part. When I am around the cynic or the crank, I am so peppy and positive that they need insulin after five minutes with me. It is so disturbing for people who hate everything to be around someone who loves everything. I figure between the two of us we make one normal person. I raise my happiness level to match their misery level, even going so far as to try to make them sing a little happy song with me. It's ridiculous. But a little "in your face" glee is just what these folks need. They say isn't it awful about the new dress code; I say it's perfect and it goes with everything I own. They say Joe is an idiot, I say Joe is so nice and he cares so much. They say the sky is falling; I say the blue will be good with their eyes. It just cracks me up. Try it.

THE GOOD NEWS

If the cranks have gotten to you, the good news will be that everything is a misery so there is lots to talk about. If they haven't, the good news is that there is good news. Not everything is awful. You'll have a balanced view of work, both good and bad stuff happens, and you just work through it all. Strangely, even the worst-case crank is attracted to someone who is positive, and these people will be on your side, even if they never ever admit it.

THE LOSER: AN EASY TARGET

There is one in every office. A dork, a weirdo, a loser. A loser says the wrong thing at every social gathering. He probably wears a bow tie, or a bow in her hair or something goofy. He might be too perky or too gloomy or too smart or too dumb. He is too something; there's no doubt about that. Maybe he looks like a normal person, but he walks in the room and you sense he is a leper. If everyone is going out for beers and the goat comes too, you'll just want to poke out your eyes. It's just your horrid luck that he'll probably sit next to you too.

Road Rule #85: *It is not about being "in"; it's about results.*

The office goat can't do anything right. And if you aren't sure what's really wrong with him everyone else in the office will be glad to point out every awful little thing he does, like wearing those pants. Or possibly he likes to tell silly jokes or say corny phrases. Maybe it's his haircut. Or he's talkative. All of which we know are capital offenses.

THE BAD NEWS

The age-old problems of group-sponsored meanness aren't left behind in the playground. Group meanness is very easy to practice in the workplace. *Practice* may be the wrong word; it's natural to have someone to spit on. Or is it? So, when the office goat appears, you would be better off stepping back and making up your own mind about this person. What is the point of being a grown-up if you don't get to make up your own mind about people?

WHAT YOU CAN DO

Is it really necessary to roll your eyes when he comes in and says "Good morning, morning glory"? It's drippy, I know, but is it really so awful that you have to punish someone for it? Is it required to mutter "Oh, no" every time the Lord of Goofballs approaches you? It's not. No matter what anyone else does, you know what's mean. So does the drip, by the way.

You might even find that if you are nice to this poor dorky soul, he turns out to be a nice person—and smart, too. I'm not suggesting that you have to adopt him. You don't have to take anyone on as a personal project if you don't want to. You don't have to like everyone. But if you want to be treated with respect, you'll have to start. There is the old saying, You have to be cruel to be kind. But it isn't true. You have to be kind to be kind, and cruel is just cruel.

I'm no fool. I know perfectly well that if you are the only person who goes out of your way to be decent to the office dork that the dork will be on you like Elmer's on a collage. If it were easy to be nice to everyone, everyone would be nice. But keep in mind: In a company where they target people to be hated, what's to keep them from picking on you next?

THE GOOD NEWS

Remember, if the culture needs a goat, they'll pick anyone. Even you. But rise above the crowd here, and people will respect you for it. You are not going to be able to work only with cool, groovy people just like you. It's best to focus on people's results rather than on their personalities. It saves you lots of energy and keeps you feeling like a fine, upstanding person.

WHAT IF IT'S YOU?

I hope it doesn't happen, but you may find that you are the office goat. You step out of the room and touch your nose to see if there is a big booger hanging off it, because everyone giggled at everything you said. You slip into the bathroom periodically during the day to sniff under your arms to see if you smell and constantly check your zipper. You must be doing something to be treated like a worm on the salad. I wish I could tell you why this happens. When a company lets people be treated like dirt, someone is going to have to be the dirt. It always seems sort of random. I've studied office goats and I can't figure out what makes someone not fit in other than small-mindedness on someone's part.

It really can happen to anyone. Stop beating yourself up immediately. One thing I know won't work is trying hard to fix it. This is not your problem to fix. Just focus on doing a good job at work and find like-minded people to hang out with outside the office. If someone is nice to you, don't cling to him like the life preserver that they are. Be nice in return and imagine an arm always between you. It's simply best to let people come to you. If they do they do, if they don't they don't. Their loss. It really is. Keep doing a good job and start looking around for another job. You need to get to an environment where there are decent people to work with as soon as possible. If you stay where you are you'll be beaten down, and no job is worth it. The people you are working with certainly are not worth it. I know I sound like your mom here. I only resort to these tactics because your mother was right.

THE YACK MACHINE

You have a big deadline. It's 8:00 P.M. and you have at least one more hour's work to do. You can't go home until the project is complete. Suddenly you hear the *Jaws* theme in the air. Duh Dum. Duh Dum. It builds. You look up. Oh no! The talking time eater is gliding like a shark toward your desk. You know that once this person gets talking, she can't stop. You try to look frazzled, she starts talking about what she had for breakfast. You give short, brief "uh huh's" for responses. You look longingly at the pile of papers on your desk as your palms begin to sweat. The talker begins to list all her best friends according to height for some reason. You don't know why. In your mind you let go a silent scream. She has to repeat the list several times to get it just right. You mention that you sure have a lot to do. She tells you how much she has to do too and how she is going to do it and what she'll wear, think and feel as she does it. You get glassy-eyed and wonder if you'd be put on notice if you strangled a coworker.

THE BAD NEWS

There are people in every office whose sole responsibility seems to be to walk around and talk to people for hours at a time. These folks are completely insensitive to the idea that you may actually have some work to do as they sit down in your cubicle guest chair and settle in for a good long conversation.

Yappers stop by to ask you a simple question and forty-five minutes later they wander off to annoy someone else. When the office yapper walks away, you wonder if there are any openings in his department because he doesn't seem to have much to do.

Often the conversations are about work, so it doesn't feel so much like wasting time. Sometimes when things are slow, you even welcome this person because he does have lots of interesting things to talk about. After about forty-five minutes discussing possible company strategies, you still have the same amount of work to do. The end of the day begins to seem further and further away.

WHAT YOU CAN DO

This is probably a nice person and you don't want to appear rude. Again, you may even welcome his conversation sometimes, so you don't want him to hate you and never speak to you again. So you sit, half listening, and feel your blood pressure rise.

Road Rule #86: *You get to manage your time.*

You actually can and should tell this person to get lost sometimes. But you don't say, "Get out! I'm loosing my mind! Shut up and go away"—even if that is what you are thinking. What you can say is, "I've got a killer deadline here, and I've got to get back to it right now if I'm going to make my deadline. I'll talk to you later." Smile, turn around fast, pick up the phone. Dial with one hand and wave good-bye with the other. It's perfectly acceptable and expected. Even the worst talker says OK and wanders off to talk with someone else.

I've never offended someone by politely saying I have to get back to work. I have offended people by not saying anything and looking at the papers, the ceiling, rolling my eyes, and grimacing. So just say it. They'll be fine. You, on the other hand, won't have to explain that the deadline was missed because you were talking.

THE GOOD NEWS

If you take control of this situation, you will be well on the road to learning to manage your time. This is the big challenge in all work environments. People write books about it, take classes in it and write computer programs to teach it. It's this simple. When someone or something is eating your precious time away, cut it out. You'll pay for it in midnight oil if you don't.

THE FUSSBUDGET

Some people like things "just so." They like them so "just so" that it drives you crazy. Not only is it impossible to please them; every time you don't cross that *T*, they behave as if the entire organization is going to hell in a handbasket and it's all your fault. Freud would call these people anal retentive; you just think they are a pain in the butt.

Road Rule #87: *Someone has to be fussy.*

Fussbudgets are generally the people who make you do things that you don't care about in a way that you don't care to do them. They are comfortable doing things only one way, and it really messes with their mind to experience anything in a new way. These were kids who always made their bed, put their toys away and always wore cardigan sweaters. Sometimes it's a not-seeing-the-forest-for-the-trees thing and sometimes they are completely right. When they are right is when they really get under your skin.

THE BAD NEWS

Fussbudgets don't believe they are fussy; they believe in a one true way for everything. If the goldenrod copy is to go to them, they will not be able to accept the green copy even if the information is all the same. It's goldenrod or it's wrong. Don't try to tell a fussbudget that it doesn't really matter, because for them it's all that matters.

Often fussy people gravitate to jobs where they have to approve things like forms and reports. This means unless you fill out the form just right they will purse their lips really tightly and send it back to you. If you ignore them, they will develop flop sweat on their upper lip and complain about you bitterly to anyone who will listen. The thing about a fussbudget is that it is easier to let him be right than to try to reason with him. So understand that you will lose.

WHAT YOU CAN DO

Like I said, the thing about a fussbudget is that it is easier to let him be right than to try to reason with him. And before you start screaming or mocking him, remember that he is right. Sometimes things need to be done properly and completely. Even if you don't see it, someone has put the fusspot in the job to do just what he is doing. He isn't going to stop being fussy just because you find it annoying.

Often the people who make you go crazy by wanting things a certain way want them that way because there are implications to doing things wrong that you haven't even imagined. You only think they are fussy because they aren't very good at explaining the implications, so they get pissy about everything. Alas, that's your problem.

THE GOOD NEWS

You can win these people over, though, even if you can never change them. First recognize that nearly everyone they come into contact with pushes back and puts up a futile fight. So when they ask for something to be corrected, just go ahead and do it. This is confusing to them. Also, if you turn in a form early from time to time they love you for it.

If you ask for your anal-retentive friends' opinion about a procedure you are trying to figure out, they can come up with important steps that you wouldn't have thought about until they weren't done and it's midnight and you are experiencing what they call a complete disaster. It's their job to make sure that things are right, so let them do their job. If you get that steel trap mind on your side, you can save yourself a lot of heartache.

If this person has taught you to do it right the first time, you have learned a very valuable lesson. Sometimes the only way to get people to do it right is to make it harder for them to do it wrong. Fussbudgets know this, so they are relentless. If you can be half as meticulous as this person who is driving you mad, you'll go far. Cross those *T*s and learn.

THE GRUDGE MATCH

Ya hate 'em. Ya just can't stand 'em. Everything about them gives you the creeps. They are rotten, unfair, unthinking, out to get you and, by golly, you are going to get them first, the lousy rat fink pig-dogs. They have ruined your life. It's a fight to the finish. Careful, because the finish might just be yours.

Or, try the scene in reverse. You are a happy well-adjusted person, and for no reason at all in the world this person just seems out to get you. It's clear they despise you, but they are so slippery about it. You get e-mail in the morning pointing out some horror you have committed. The memo is copied to your boss and anyone else who is important in the company. This is one vicious, ruthless hunter and you are her prey.

THE BAD NEWS

As I've said, you don't have to like everyone you work with, and they don't have to like you. Still, what do you do when you just hate someone or she hates you? This can wreck a perfectly good job for you. Soon you're looking in your closet every morning to figure out what armor and chain mail to wear instead of which shirt. Pretty soon, you are looking for poison rings and strange curses to inflict. It is a waste of time for you and, more important, for your managers whom you try to drag into the conflict for protection. It's a waste of the company's time.

This sort of thing takes your mind off accomplishing anything that the company is actually paying you to do and focuses your attention on warfare. If you jump into the personal-vendetta pool, make sure you know how to swim. The truth is, sooner or later management will get sick of putting up with you and your enemy and it's curtains for you both.

WHAT YOU CAN DO

No one bothers to hate anyone she works with unless there is a threat of some sort. You may be threatened that she will try to take your job. She might be threatened that you will expose her as the complete moron that she is. There is always a threat. Figure out what that is, and attack it, not the person. You can conquer all. When you are the hater and not the hate-ee, it's easier to do the right thing. You can or should have some control over yourself. Even when there is mutual despising going on, you get to manage yourself.

Road Rule #88: *Fight about the work, not your coworkers.*

The first thing to remember when you really hate someone you work with is this: bummer. No one really cares that you find this person to be the fingernails on the chalkboard of your life. If you have compelling business reasons to be concerned about this person, then speak to your manager about it. A compelling reason is something like you saw him take home the petty cash box, or he has mailed the business plan to a major competitor. That he is snippy, rude and smells like a day-old egg salad sandwich are not compelling business reasons. Everyone knows that he is snippy, rude and smells of old egg salad and yet, he must be contributing something. Let others figure out what to do about it. If you hate someone because he is threatening to you, remember it is your good work that will win out, not your conniving. Someday you'll be the manager and you won't have to put up with these kinds of people.

Don't pick fights; don't tell him every little thing he does is wrong. Don't give him the evil eye as you pass in the rest room. Be polite, be professional, and go home and write short stories where he ends up working in some muddy ditch somewhere or something. Even better, say to yourself, "Sure, he is slime, but in the scheme of life he doesn't matter at all." You'll be right.

Now, if you are the despise-ee, it's a little tougher. I will begin with that powerful mantra, "Sure, they hate me, but in the scheme of my life, they matter not at all." Say this a lot when people hate you, and it will keep them from becoming complete monsters in your mind. If they become big and scary in your own mind, they are well on their way to winning this war. Don't ever believe they are right about you and don't ever get defensive.

Try to figure out what it is about you that threatens them. Perhaps they want your job. Perhaps they see you are smarter than they are or people like you more. When you understand what scares them about you, try not to pour salt in their wounds, as satisfying as that may be. It just makes the situation worse. Proceed if everything is as it should be.

It's never been true that when someone hated me, sooner or later, I didn't return the feeling. When that happens it's very important for you to grab control of yourself and not add fuel to the fire. If you have an enemy, never let her know that you understand that she hates you. This forces her underground, and she is more dangerous when you can't see what she is up to. It's useful to play pleasant as pie and dumb as a brick. It keeps your enemy out in the open where everyone can keep an eye on her. Pretty soon someone will see what she is up to and you'll have your first important ally.

The second important trick is to take her very literally at her word. Never guess the obvious hidden meaning behind her snipes. Look like a sweet angel and ask what she means by suggesting that "It's really very simple but of course you could never do it." If you don't bite she'll stop spoon-feeding you, and she'll look bad in the process. Repeat in a pleasant way the hateful things she says to you in private. Wait till your boss and young Machiavelli are all together and say "Machiavelli here mentioned yesterday that I am not worth the air I breathe. What are your thoughts, chief?" This is hilarious comedy and makes you look smart and amused. Your adversary looks like the creep she is. If you start to bite back, pretty soon management will be fed up with both of you. You'll both be risking your job when that happens.

THE GOOD NEWS

Here is a rule I go by that has saved my life. When I hate one person, I can figure out what to do about it and move on. I'll try the direct approach first, and then keep figuring out a way around the wall. If I hate two people, I tread very carefully, because I may be the problem. If I hate three or more people at the same time, it's definitely me, so I'd better go off in a corner somewhere and get over myself.

DIVERSITY IN THE WORKPLACE

Did you feel that rush your first day in the office? That was your socioeconomic world being blown open. While you were in school, as different as everyone appeared, most people you encountered had a lot in common with you. They had the same education, they were the same age, and more often than not they probably had a lot of the same values you do. Now you're in the big world, and the difficulty is that it is full of so many people. The best thing you can do is open your mind and heart and take as much of the good stuff home with you as you can. Sort of like going to Paris and returning with a new appreciation for snails.

Road Rule #89: *Your coworkers don't have to see the world the way you do.*

It is easy to believe that everyone else believes all the stuff you believe. If you hang around with the same kind of people long enough, everything sounds logical. When you start a new job, however, you'll find that a lot of the people you are working with believe in a completely different world view. Their experiences and perspectives are just as valid as yours. That is called diversity. Everyone you work with doesn't have to be like you or see the world the way you do.

Road Rule #90: *Check your "isms" at the office door.*

You are going to have to check all your "isms" at the door. Racism and sexism exists in the workplace, there is no denying it. A large part of it happens when people confuse their perspectives with realities. Remember: Most of us grew up with people like us, whose experiences in life are like ours. These people have given us our perspective about how things are. But our experiences aren't everyone else's. If any of your coworkers and managers are women or are from a different race than you, it's probably time to check your assumptions and accept new perspectives.

If you have difficulties working for any kind of person you can categorize as "not you," bear in mind that it is your difficulty and you'll have to be the one to overcome it. Most companies are full of people with backgrounds different from yours. Your old prejudices will say more about you than they ever will about anyone else.

Diversity is a lot more than "accepting" people from different backgrounds as long as they act like you. There is no one right way to approach a problem; there is no one right way to get the job done or even to behave. There is plenty to learn from people who aren't like you. People who are just exactly like you may make you more comfortable, but you'll have a richer life if you decide to be challenged with new people and ideas and approaches.

No matter how deeply you believe in your theories about anyone else's race, age, gender, religion or sexual orientation, those are your personal issues and they don't belong in the workplace. Here's the world, and all sorts of us are in it. Get used to it. You might even enjoy it.

If you go to England and you keep driving on the right side of the road, you aren't going to get very far—even if you know that it is better, safer and just plain right to drive on the right side of the road. You are going to have to make adjustments for the millions of people who don't think you are right.

At the same time, you will find that you may be the recipient of other people's "isms" throughout your career. And when that happens, you need to think very carefully about how you want to handle it. Remember, you don't have to put up with it. Still it's hard to figure out how to make the behavior stop. I would suggest that you see the human resources manager right away if you believe you are being treated unfairly because of age, race, sex or religion. Prejudicial behavior is illegal, and most companies aren't going to mess around with it.

You and the personnel manager should figure out a course of action that you are comfortable with. That may range anywhere from you or the human resources manager discussing this person's behavior with him, to asking for an apology, to terminating the person. This will depend on what has happened and what you think is the right thing to do. You should be prepared to discuss what you believe to be a fair course of action. The law requires that a company provide a nonhostile work environment for all its employees, so they must take some action on your part.

CORPORATE CULTURES

The things that everyone you work with do have in common, like work ethics and the way you treat one another, are called a corporate culture. Do people in corner offices matter more than others? Is it OK to yell at someone in front of everyone? Does everyone go out and play together? What kind of behavior does the company reward, and what kind do they punish? These are the things that make up a corporate culture. You don't have to buy into everything you find in your company's culture. You just have to learn not to tread on too many of the company's sacred behaviors.

Road Rule #91: *Understand what the company values.*

It's worth a reminder that the clues to sacred behaviors are found in sentences that begin with: "In the old days . . . ," "We always . . . ," "We never . . . ," ". . . always says." Clues are also found in the behavior of the people who are successful in the company. Are they friendly or are they very buttoned up? You don't have to be a stiff to survive in a buttoned-up culture; you can be friendly and buttoned up. Are the big dogs standoffish to the worker bees, or do they build teams? It is as important to manage yourself "down and around" as it is to manage yourself "up." That is, the wider the sphere of influence you have, the more support and ultimate success you'll find.

Road Rule #92: *You must influence yourself first.*

In order to influence others, you need to understand what makes someone a leader in the company you work for. You don't have to be a capitalist pig dog to succeed; you can be a leader, not a dictator. In order not to become the biggest kiss-up on the planet, make sure you look around, too—not just up.

Within a corporate culture there are all sorts of rules, unwritten and written, that determine how everyone behaves toward one another. The fastest way to figure out the unwritten ones is to look around and pay attention. Who gets fired? Who gets promoted? Are the people you think are smart in the boardroom or in the basement? If they are in the basement, you might not have the cultural fit you'll want in order to succeed here.

A good place to find out the written rules of the corporate culture is in the company handbook. There you'll find all the rules that someone thinks and hopes people are following. It's a good idea to know what these rules are, because you don't want to break them. If you do, that can mean termination for "cause." Termination for cause means no unemployment for you. After you read the handbook, look around and see if anyone is following the rules, just in case.

During the course of your career, you'll have to work with and for all sorts of people. You don't have to like all of them, but then they don't pay you to like anyone. Still, it's much nicer if you can. When you don't like someone you work with, then it's time to concentrate on what they do, what they contribute and achieve, and leave personalities alone.

12
ETIQUETTE: To Party, or Not to Party

SOCIAL SKILLS. GOTTA HAVE 'EM. I KNOW A WONDERFUL AND SMART YOUNG MAN WHOSE CAREER STALLED OUT because when food was served at a meeting, this strapping youth would eat half the sandwiches on the tray as fast as he could and then top them off with a couple of sixteen-ounce sodas. Sure, he was hungry. What was the problem? He was at a business meeting, not a pie-eating contest. That was the problem. People were so amazed at his ability to breathe in a roast-beef sandwich that they never paid any attention to his ideas.

Road Rule #93: *Table manners count.*

If you have manners, no one notices; if you don't have them, everyone notices and wonders how careful you are with their work as the mayonnaise soaks into your shirt. They will certainly not invite you to those client meetings and dinners you've been hoping to get in on. Think of it this way: Not talking with your mouth full can give you valuable time to think of brilliant things to say.

Again, I know of a very senior person whose star was rising in the company, until the president of the company went out to lunch with him. His slurping and chomping so offended the president that his star began to fall. He was never allowed at a client dinner without someone else there to balance out those manners, and he never had a meal with the president again. One of the worst things about working for a living is discovering how many times your parents were right.

At any meeting where food is served, the focus should be on the agenda and not on the free grub. Even if your first job isn't paying you very much, even if you are living on mac and cheese, you don't want people to think that you haven't eaten in a week. Restraint—management loves restraint. Screaming out, "Oh goodie, cookies!" and leaping across the table may not portray the professional image you'd like. You should fill your plate with what everyone else would consider a reasonable portion. Then after everyone else has had some, go for a little bit more if you are dying. Maybe splurge with a second cookie. But don't eat like a ranch hand unless you happen to be working at a ranch. There are no grandmas in the room to be delighted about your healthy appetite. Another of my secret tips is to make friends with the caterers, and then they'll save you something extra for after the meetings.

It's just the same with business dinners. You don't have to order the meat loaf in a fine restaurant, but you don't want to take advantage either. Even if you are paying for it, ordering by price shows that you are not cavalier with money, especially not your money, possibly even their money. Order what you want, treat yourself some, but be reasonable. You can have a drink if you are so inclined and even have the fruit compote or better for dessert. If everyone is drinking more than a few, make sure you aren't the drunkest one there. Waking up and finding you have lots of explaining to do is a miserable moment. Avoid it. Anytime you are with a business associate or client, even if it is after hours, your professionalism is being watched.

Company parties can be tricky. If you hate parties, is it OK never to go? If you love parties, are you in danger of being the company barfly? Well, in a big way it depends on where you work. How people party together is a clue to the corporate culture. Some companies believe in enforced fun: you aren't part of the team if you don't attend nearly every function that they throw. Other companies don't care much, but usually there is one event a year that is a "must attend," often the holiday party. If you don't like parties much, your best bet is to go to the first couple and pay attention to who's there and who's not. If everyone whom you want to kiss up to is at every hullabaloo every time, then you might want to be there just about every time too. You don't have to go with a capital *H* have to, but it doesn't hurt if you show up from time to time and pretend to enjoy yourself. You can stop by and bail out early, saying you have something else you have to do that evening.

Road Rule #94: *At the company party never get drunker than the "big cheese."*

Parties can be a great time to bond with your superiors and coworkers, so take advantage. If you are really lucky, your boss will be the one with the morning regrets. If you don't like her very much, it can be a very satisfying experience: one that you won't want to miss. If the crowd changes from shindig to shindig, then do what you will.

If you just love to party, watch the level on the hilarity scale very carefully. They may call it a party, but it is not the same as going on a tear with your pals. A company party is really just business with cocktails. You don't want to be the only one on the conga line. Sure it's a party, but people will take their impressions back to the office the next day. It is absolutely true that people might not remember the names of half of the junior vice presidents that have come and gone from a company, but stories about people who humiliated themselves at a company party become legends.

Whatever happens, don't be drunker than the big cheese. One of my old bosses used to bring out her Polaroid camera when she'd had a few. Pretty soon she'd start snapping pictures of everyone. That was the signal for the rest of us to go ahead and break the fun meter.

CHAPTER 13

GET a Life!

Y OU ARE FOCUSED ON YOUR CAREER. YOU MAY EVEN READ BOOKS ABOUT CAREERS, THE LATEST TRICKS IN management or the buzzwords. Every move could make or break you. Hell, you don't have time to think about your personal life. You aren't a person anymore; you are an employee, damn it! You are one of the few, the proud, the employed. Well, remember that one of the obligations to your employer is to be at your best, have a positive attitude, be efficient and not burn out. If they have to check you in to the Peaceful Hills Rest Home, then they are going to have to hire and train someone all over again. Really, it's thoughtless of you not to have a life. I'm afraid you are simply going to have to make sure that you take care of yourself.

Full-time work can be a pretty intense thing compared to school or anything else you've encountered so far. Unlike classes, you don't get to cut memos when you feel like it. You don't get to schedule your day to start at 11 A.M. so that you can party all night. Worst of all, the semester doesn't end until you are sixty-five. They actually expect you to show up every day, on time, get something done, and not leave until 5 P.M. This seems outrageous, I know, and actually some places are changing this routine. Virtual offices and telecommuting are becoming more commonplace. But even in these environments, you are expected to be on top of everything every day. There is very little you can cram the night before your work is due. When you do, it shows. While just passing may have still gotten you a diploma, it won't ever give you a raise or a promotion.

Work can be a very seductive thing. It is where you spend most of your waking hours, and after you've graduated, it is where you will meet more new people than you will anywhere else. It is easy to talk about it all the time, go out with coworkers to talk about work all the time, party with coworkers to talk about it all the time and hang out with friends from work on the weekends to talk about work all the time. It's what you gossip about, worry about, plan about. And pretty soon that's all there is to you.

So how do you get through it? You get a life! Take a class. Get a hobby. Learn to paint. Take up pottery or white-collar boxing. Discover cooking . . . Well, that seems like a desperate move to me.

A good rule is to have three different things going on in your life. Work, relationships and hobbies; or work, sports and volunteerism; or work, school and cooking. You get it. But it's important. If you have three things going on, there will be at least one thing in your life that isn't poop. When work is bad and that's your whole life, then your whole life will seem bad. You won't have the perspective you'll need to figure out what do to. Sometimes work stinks and you are on a losing baseball team. If you can cook or paint or write or something, you have a place to retreat to. I've just told you one of life's great secrets. Don't spread it around.

Road Rule #95: *Balance your life so you don't burn out.*

If you have changed cities for your job, it can be a difficult prospect to get a life. For a long time your energies will be spent figuring out how to get to and from work, where to buy groceries, where to live and how to keep your job. Consequently the path of least resistance is to have your whole life grow out of the place where you go every day. There are lots of resources there, and you should take advantage of them. Join the baseball team if there is one. Join the holiday party committee. Invite yourself out for a beer when you see a bunch of people going out. But sooner or later, you're going to need to develop friends and resources outside the workplace. Most cities offer adult-education classes or art classes and have tons of "interest" clubs. You don't have to be good at any of it. Happily, your real life doesn't get graded or reviewed.

Getting a life is even harder if you are one of the lucky ones who love their job and their company. If the people you work with are the coolest people on the planet, why would you want to waste your time with all the losers who don't work with you? Because sooner or later you'll hit a bad patch and you'll be without any resources. Even in the best companies, there are periods with bad morale. As much as you love what you do, you'll have lousy assignments or lousier managers from time to time. If you haven't developed other resources for yourself, you'll be in hell every day from nine to five and then go home to your pathetic life to dwell on being in hell every day from nine to five. Find a book club; they are posted in most bookstores. Find a choral group, start a UFO-sightings club. It's your life; fill it up. When you are taking your last breaths at the end of it all, will you look back on the proposal you worked so hard on that you couldn't go out, or the people and activities you filled your life with? If it's the first, you'll need to get a personality too. A friend's mom says the cemeteries are filled with people who believed that work just couldn't get along without them.

Road Rule #96: *Keep in touch with your industry and the rest of the world.*

It's also a good idea to know what's happening in the world and in your industry. This is called citizenship. I know it sounds corny. But now you are one of those stupid adults you keep pointing at asking why they don't do something about the world. Keeping abreast of the news and your industry will help you bring in fresh ideas to work and to your life. It will help you to understand changing policies and issues. Unless your first job out of school is ambassador to Cuba or something, the fate of the world does not ride on what you are doing—no matter how much everyone else at the company believes that it does. But the fate of your world might rely on your vote or on your ability to foresee trends or new opportunities in your industry. It might depend on your deciding to get out of the office to do some small thing about this wacky planet.

Even if you really love art, when planning your trip,

make sure that you schedule more than museum after museum. If you don't, you'll hate all art by the end of the
week—and you'll have missed out on a lot of other good
things that the world has to offer.

CHAPTER **14**

MANAGING Yourself as a New Manager

YOU WERE BORN FOR THIS. YOU ARE A NATURAL LEADER OF PEOPLE. YOU HAVE CONFIDENCE AND AN understanding air about you. You will be firm but kind, just like Maria von Trapp on her way to meet those little singing children. Ha! That's a sucker's dream. Before you get too full of yourself, go back and read the chapter on getting along with your boss. The people you are now in charge of are thinking you are one of those people; there is no doubt about it.

There are millions of books on management, and this is not one of them. I can give you a few tips to avoid some common blunders until you get a chance to get to the bookstore. In a sentence: Most new managers try to control too much and actually manage too little.

Road Rule #97: *When you become a manager, don't forget to make time to manage.*

You got promoted because you know how to DO. Doing is what you do well, so you do want to keep doing it. But it's not just do do do anymore. In this world nobody just manages; you have to produce, too. Part of what you have to do now is help others to do, too.

Be prepared for this new wonderful world. But be warned. If you are managing people who were once your coworkers, they will give you a run for your money. They will be much harder to manage than new people, even if (especially if) they were your good pals before. If you are firm, they will think you've become a megalomaniac. If you are too soft and friendly, they will take complete advantage of you and you'll wonder why you are doing their work and your work too. One or the other and often both at the same time will happen to you. It always does. So err on the side of being firm. The hard news to take is you aren't their pal anymore, you are their supervisor. The truth is everyone wants a supervisor they know is in charge, even if they try to sabotage you. It's a test. You can only pass it by becoming the person in charge. While everyone has to adjust to your new role, make sure that you remember it's your job to see they do their job. You don't need to turn into a control freak, and if you try you'll go nuts. Set goals and objectives for your staff, give clear directions, give clear directions again, and then let 'em go to it. Correct them when they are wrong, and praise what they do well.

Next, remember that part of your job as manager means that you have to spend some time actually managing. Managing means explaining, teaching, reviewing other people's work and delegating. It's calming people down, pumping them up and listening. At the end of the day, you can't point to any of these things and say, "Look what I did." For a doer like you, this is troubling at first. A manager is a guide, a parent, a counselor, a principal and a taskmaster, and good ones are mentors. It is easy to think of this as unproductive and a waste of time. If you spend some of your day managing others, you may have fewer pieces of paper in your out-box at the end of the day, but it doesn't mean you haven't accomplished a lot.

You are used to doing tasks, and you do them well or you wouldn't have been promoted. But the time you spend seeing how your new staff is doing, showing them how to do it better, and correcting their work makes for more efficiencies for everyone. That means more time and more happiness. You need feedback. Everyone on your staff will, too, so you've got to watch what's going on so that you can give directions to your staff. A simple tip that can give you lifelong loyalty from your staff: Compliment them in front of people and reprimand them in private. When you give people credit in front of others, it gives them bragging rights, and feels even better. If someone messes up, never humiliate him or her in front of others. People don't get over it. Always let them know in private what's not going well, and keep the conversation private unless the behavior continues.

It may feel easier just to do everything yourself rather than to take the time to teach the people who are working for you to do it. Most new managers do this. They know they can do the work, but they don't know how to help someone else to do it. Rather than showing someone, they end up just doing it themselves. But remember how eager you were to get your hands on more interesting stuff when you started out? If you keep it all to yourself, you aren't being fair to the people who work for you. Delegate. You have to, or you'll be at the rest home before you can say "deadline."

Road Rule #98: *Managing people would be easier without the people.*

If you have been promoted to supervise the job you once had, don't compare the work of the person you are now supervising to your amazing performance in the role. You probably have no idea what a goof you were when you first started. You just remember how great you were by the time they decided to promote you. Instead, compare yourself to the best manager you ever had. Ask yourself what she would have done in this situation, then try to do the same. I'll bet the best manager you had didn't try to do everything or hold things close to the vest. She gave you feedback. She challenged you with work that seemed over your head. She let you find your own best way to get the work done well. Your instincts will be to do the opposite. Your instincts will be to just do it all, or to overcontrol the process or criticize if it wasn't done exactly the way you would have done it. For heaven's sake, don't pay attention to your instincts. There is almost nothing instinctual or natural about managing others.

Road Rule #99: *You can't control everything, and it is a poor manager who tries.*

Lots of your staff will be great, but you'll also have ones who are not so great. There will be those who are difficult to deal with or who just can't quite hack it. Don't beat up on yourself if some of the people who work for you don't have the work ethic or common sense you have. You can't "manage" your staff into being better or smarter than they are. Don't try to cover for them or put up with them. In the long run it will reflect badly on you for not doing something about it. Get some advice from a mentor or another manager. Find out what the company's notice and termination policies are. I was once told that no one will believe that a new manager is really in charge until he fires someone. This is not to say you should come in your first day with a big ax, but managing includes terminating people, too. Just be sure when you sit down and tell someone that she is "outta here" that you know you've done all you could. You should be confident that this person got clear instructions from you that weren't followed. As you walk in the room to change someone's life, you need to be able to remind yourself of the many chances and clear warnings this person got from you.

If you have problem employees, and you will, get the advice of human resources or your own boss. It is very likely that at some point you'll become concerned about someone's mental health. There may be a harassment complaint brought to you. Your employees will come to you with some pretty complex personal problems that are affecting their work. You are not expected to deal with these problems all on your own, and how you handle things may have legal implications. The human resources department or personnel should know the laws and have whatever it takes to help you and the employee.

CHAPTER 15

THE END: Quitting, Being Put on Notice, Getting Fired

YOU QUIT!

THERE ARE LOTS OF REASONS PEOPLE QUIT THEIR JOBS. WHEN YOUR PARENTS AND GRANDPARENTS STARTED working, they expected to stay in the same profession most of their careers, and possibly even with the same company. Times aren't like that anymore. Loyalty is a good thing, but business rarely sees their loyalty to you as more important than their obligation to remain in business. Sometimes you look out for yourself first, and move on. If you believe that the company is in trouble, you might want to get your resume updated and in circulation rather than sitting around waiting for the angel of death-and-termination to ask to see you in his office. If you feel you've given your heart and soul and you don't see that promotion coming, you might be able to get it at another company. And sometimes you find yourself working for a bunch of cheap mean lousy so-and-sos doing unthinkable work, and you just can't take it anymore.

Road Rule #100: *It is easier to get a new job if you currently have a job.*

If you really just hate your job, I suggest that you take a deep breath and try to get another job before you quit. This isn't always possible. I know, I've done it. But when you are interviewing for a new job, it gives you more credibility if you still have a job. It means that someone thinks you are worth paying.

When interviewing, it's best to be cautious about what you say about your current job. The people that you are interviewing with don't know your current boss. If you say that they he is a moron and unfair, they will suspect that the unfair moron might just be you. Try to impress the interviewer that you want to come to work at their company for its merits more than you want to escape from your current nightmare. If you really just can't take another minute, you can usually cough up some temp work or something if you have to leave without another job. But before you jump, remind yourself that this is only a job, not who you are. Get some perspective, do something for yourself. Say you have a dentist appointment and then really go to the movies. Give yourself the weekend to chill before you tell them to stick it.

Road Rule #101: *Don't resign unless you really mean it.*

Sometimes job offers come to you. You hear about something, a recruiter calls you or someone you used to work with will steal you away to work with her now. This is the best way and reason to leave a job. Make sure that the new place is really what you want and not just something new. Ask someone to show you around, and see if the people look happy. Ask why the position is open. Why did the last person leave the job? And make sure you will be doing the kinds of things you've been looking forward to trying. Often the best way to get a raise is to get a new job with a new company. More money can be half a good reason to quit a job, but make sure there is something else worthwhile about your new job, too.

It is considered good form to give at least two weeks' notice before you move on. Even if you hate your job, try to do this. It is better not to burn any bridges you may need to cross again. While you may never want to work in that dump again, there may be people there that you might want to work for sometime. Two weeks allows everyone to get over the shock and start to find your replacement. It will allow you to clean up any loose ends, show someone your unique filing system and pass on any projects to someone else. If you've been very good it also gives them time to plan your going-away party. One company I worked for threw such good going-away parties that I quit there three different times.

Don't be surprised if people are upset with you when you quit: not only because now they have to go through the hassle of replacing you, but also because you've just told them that you don't want to be in their club anymore. This hurts their very sensitive feelings and gentle natures. I've seen lots of bosses who feel personally rejected when their employees quit. They are pretty cold and unpleasant for a few days. Try to be kind. They'll get over it, and then if you hate your new job, you can ask for your old one back.

Sometimes you will get a counteroffer: your current company likes you so much that they are going to do what they should have done for you in the first place and give you a lovely raise. Tread carefully in counteroffer territory. If they are counteroffering because you have them over some sort of barrel, they won't forget it, and it usually leads to trouble later. People resent being in the position of doing whatever it takes to keep someone, and once the crisis is over, they often come after you. If they really just love your guts out, then make sure you remember all the reasons why you decided to leave in the first place. If it was simply money that motivated your new job-hunt and they are going to match it, fine. If it was power and prestige, respect and opportunity, chances are you won't get it where you are or you would have had it already. Remember, if you accept a counteroffer, you are going to close the door on the other place for a long time. Usually when people accept a new position, they are ready to leave. Don't let your stroked ego make you choose something you'll regret when life gets back to normal. Be very sure of what you want next before you give notice in the first place.

Once everyone has the tragic news of your impending escape, contact personnel and find out if they are missing any time sheets/expense reports or documents that might hold up your final check. Sometimes it takes awhile to get on your new payroll; be very careful to save this last check. Go over the questions listed in the following work sheet to discover what else you might need to know. And if someone or several people really made a difference to you, write them thank-you notes. They'll never forget that, and they'll keep an eye out for you, even at a distance. You like to hear when you've made a difference to someone; tell someone when they've made a difference to you.

WARNING, WARNING! YOU ARE ON NOTICE!

They've warned you it would come to this; at least they think they have. Someone takes you in a room and tells you that you have thirty days to straighten out your act. They may give you as little as two weeks to stop doing whatever is making them unhappy with you. If you don't, you will be terminated. Even if you smelled this coming for months, it's still a shock when it happens. You will want to react badly; you'll feel helpless and wronged. You'll feel as though the executioner is climbing the steps to chop off your head. Don't argue or plead now. Take a deep breath and listen to what is being said to you.

When you get put on notice, one of two things is happening. They are truly trying to shock you into correcting your performance and hope that this serious step will do the trick. Or they have decided they are all done with you and are simply covering their butts legally for when they let you go at the end of the probation period. The trouble is it's hard to tell what is really going on, so it's best to play it both ways.

Road Rule #102: *If they put you on notice, update your resume right away.*

The first thing you should do is calm down. Most people get fired at least once, so it's not the worst thing in the world to happen. It really isn't. Don't flip out; do something. You should quietly update your resume. What job skills have you added since you've started this job? Get them on the resume. The third thing you should do is call some recruiters and tell them you are looking for something else. Say you aren't really happy where you are and would like to get some interviews going. Or get the help-wanted section out at home and fire off a couple of resumes. If you start to explore other options right away, you'll feel that you have some control over what happens next. No need to freeze. Don't think about it much; just get some resumes out into the world, even if you're not sure you'd want that job.

Now it's time to figure out what to do about your current job. Make sure you get a copy of the notice so that you can read it over very carefully and see if you can figure out what it is they want that they aren't getting from you. Think about this very carefully. Sometimes what they want isn't what you are good at or want to do. If this is the case, then maybe fate is taking you and kicking you back out the door to find the job you should have. Try to give them what they want while you step up your job search. It is much easier to get a new job while you have the old one. Then you don't have to answer those tricky questions about why/how you left your old position.

Road Rule #103: *Usually you can save your job if you want to.*

If you want this job and believe you can do it, go back and ask questions about anything on the notice that you don't understand. If you don't agree with what's there, don't argue, just ask for clarification. Push right out of your head those nasty conversations in your mind about how unfair this is and how wrong they are. Listen very carefully and keep trying to understand. If you ask for examples, you may be able to justify every one of them, but don't try.

Use the examples to understand this is the kind of thing that's getting you into trouble, not just that specific thing. Remember, this is another person's perception of you, not who you are. Her perception is what you need to understand. If you believe that you can give her what she wants, let your supervisor know that you understand completely what she needs and will correct your behavior or performance right away. If you do correct what are perceived as your shortcomings, keep it up, don't slack off again after a few weeks. They aren't asking for a change just during the notice or probation period. Your manager has zero tolerance now, and if he thinks you're messing up again, he won't bother with a notice. So just in case, keep the job hunt open for a while. You certainly don't need to tell potential employers that they are just about to can your behind at your current job. Talk about new challenges, and how you always wanted to work at their company. Make sure you talk about something new, challenging and exciting that you want to do.

THEY KILLED YOU FIRST! YOU GOT FIRED!

If you get fired, don't forget that this may be the first time it's happened to you, but it is certainly not the first time it has happened. People get fired all the time. Good, smart, hardworking people get fired. Sometimes they get fired for performance and sometimes they get laid off, which is a nice way of saying "We are firing you because we can't afford you anymore." Since getting fired once is likely to happen to anyone, be freed by the idea that you've gotten it over with. No one who has ever been fired was able to argue her way out of it, so even if you think it was unfair, don't bother. You would not be normal if you weren't angry or devastated or both, but try to get out of there with as much dignity as possible. This makes the supervisor think he may have been wrong, and that's much more satisfying than proving he is right by throwing a fit. If you believe you've been treated unfairly, ask for an exit interview from personnel.

If you believe you have been fired illegally, call an attorney when you get home. Employment laws vary from state to state, so do some research if you aren't sure. Don't sign anything, even if it means waiting a day for your final check. Take the paperwork home, read it carefully and make sure you aren't promising anything about future jobs or lawsuits.

Unless you have stolen the company safe or something, you are eligible for unemployment benefits, so get up bright and early the next day and get in that old unemployment line. It's a nightmare, but it's your money: go get it. Register with a temp agency so you can keep some money coming in. Get the want ads and set up some meetings with employment agencies. Go to lunch, then search your soul.

Maybe you weren't in the right company for you. Companies have a personality and so do you. Maybe you and your manager never found out how to click. Start thinking about what you need from a manager and what you need to do to get the kind of supervision you need. Sometimes you just marry the wrong person, and even if the other partner figures it out first, in the end it's better to be out of the relationship.

Road Rule #104: *Getting fired can be just the thing you need to get on the right course.*

Possibly you haven't picked the right profession. Did you like the work and feel you were good at it? Or did you always think you could like it and be good at if "if only": if only you had a different supervisor, more responsibility, less responsibility, more training . . . Very often we like the concept of an industry better than we like actually working in it. The idea of being a banker or copywriter or broker or publisher might be much nicer than the work really is. Now you know what it is really like to work in this industry. Maybe it's not for you at all. Maybe despite dreaming of this kind of job for years, you just don't like it. Most people change careers many times before they find out what they like doing and do well. Getting fired may be the way you can have the time to evaluate what it is you are doing with your life, and change it if you want.

Oh, and before you start your next job, why not read this book over again to see if there isn't somewhere you went wrong, and what you could do about it next time.

WORK SHEET #6

The They Fired Me, Those Dogs! What Should I Do Now? Work Sheet

1) Go home. Go to the movies. Call a friend and tell her she is buying.
2) Call some recruiters or employment agencies and set up meetings for early the following week.
3) Call personnel and ask a bunch of questions:

- *Am I eligible for unemployment compensation?*
- *Do you have anything I can take with me to the unemployment office?*
- *Do I get any severance pay?*
- *When can I expect my final check?*
- *Do I get a payout for my unused vacation days?*
- *When do I get paid out for any 401(k), profit sharing, etc.?*
- *Do I have any outstanding expense reports or checks?*
- *When does my insurance end?*
- *Can I take some insurance claim forms with me?*
- *Can I get some information about continuing my health insurance (COBRA)?*
- *Do you have the names of some recruiters or employment agencies that you recommend?*
- *Whose name should I give if I'm asked for a reference?*
- *May I use office equipment to update/copy my resume?*

4) Ask your friends a bunch of questions:

- *Do you know of any openings?*
- *Do you have any contacts you can call?*
- *Do you know of any employment agencies you could recommend?*
- *May I give you a copy of my resume in case you hear of anything?*

5) Ask yourself a bunch of questions:

- *Did I like my job?*
- *What did I do really well?*

- *What did I need to improve?*
- *What was my supervisor trying to tell me that I just didn't hear?*
- *What did I do that made me lose my job? (Don't cop out now, come up with something, even if you think you were totally misunderstood.)*
- *Now that I've worked in this industry, can I see myself being good at and liking the next job up the line?*
- *What kind of position do I know I don't want to take?*
- *What kind of job do I think I'll succeed at next time?*
- *What other industries are interesting to me?*
- *Would I do better in an environment that is bigger/smaller, more supervised/less supervised?*
- *What would I do differently if I could have it to do over?*
- *What skills do I have now that I didn't have when I started?*
- *What do I want to learn from my next job?*

No matter why you've left a job, it's a good idea to reflect on what you've learned and learned not to do again. If it's all their fault, think again or you will be in entry-level purgatory until you learn the lessons. Don't forget: There are always bigger and better jobs out there be ready to be great.

16

THE FUTURE: A Conclusion

HISTORICALLY, THE END OF THE MILLENNIUM IS FULL OF CHANGES, TUMULT AND CONFUSION. I'M AFRAID this one doesn't look to be very much different. Unions have weakened or lost focus. Employees are thought of as replaceable and disposable. On the one hand what had seemed in the eighties to be big, giant, stable companies are now laying off people in huge numbers. On the other hand, lots of workers are dropping out of the career track in order to have balanced lives. The good news is that new kinds of companies are sprouting up all over the place. Telecommunications companies, software companies, Web companies, and small cottage industries are popping up everywhere and they are scrambling for good people.

Your career will have possibilities that you can't even imagine right now. It's the old saying "when a window closes, someone opens up a door." You will spend a good portion of your career looking for those doors that have never existed before. You won't be able to manage the marketplace, the economy or technological changes, but you can learn to manage yourself and your goals. You might as well laugh at the rest.

The roads will change a lot before you get to retire. You can take off in a lot of different directions, but you've got to get on the road and master the rules first. Your first job is just the place to do that. You can learn what you do well and what you like to do. It's likely that these are the same thing. You can find out what kind of worker you are in a place where there is less at stake. You can experiment to find out what you don't have a talent for or what you don't like to do. As you start out, you can learn to make a habit of analyzing different people and situations. In the era of the disposable worker, you'll need to learn how to make every step a very smart one.

Road Rule #105: *Keep reinventing your career.*

Once you've learned a few different plans of attack and mastered your timing, you can go anywhere you want to. You can have a traditional career (if there are any left) or invent new jobs that suit you best. When you keep a mental list of what you like to do and do well, it's like having a career compass. This list is the job description for the perfect new position. If that job doesn't exist, you can invent it. If you've mastered the basics, you'll be able to follow the map or blaze new trails.

Road Rule #106: *Learn from the soft lessons so you don't have to learn the hard ones.*

Making a success of your first job is going to be one of the hardest parts of your wild career. It feels like anyone can do this work, and honestly just about anyone can. That's why it's so tricky. But if you look for the "soft" lessons, the things that aren't so obvious, you'll feel plenty challenged. During your first job, everything is new. Not only do you have to figure out how to keep working without that semester break, but you've also got to understand a new culture, new people and new agendas. During your first job you'll be able to master skills a lot more complicated and rewarding than making copies. After this first time in the workforce it's just going to be variations on a theme. There will always be bosses. Timing always matters. You'll be making first impressions over and over again. If you apply some of the basic skills you can learn between taking phone messages, they will apply to boss after boss, position after position and company after company.

This can be the job where you create the foundation of your career. It's when you stare at all the maps and figure out where you'd like to go. No one can tell you which roads to follow. That is going to depend on your interests, curiosity and what new paths present themselves along the way. But there are going to be so many options for you. If you've packed your bags well, you'll be prepared for all kinds of weather and any road conditions. Even the bumpy roads can take you where you want to go. If you believe that this is all a big adventure, you'll have a wonderful trip. I hope you have a fun and exciting journey.

APPENDIX: Benefits, Insurance and the Law

INSURANCE AND BENEFITS:
A PRIMER

If you have graduated from school and/or are over twenty-four years old, you may no longer be eligible as a dependent on your parents' insurance policies. This means you will need to take any insurance that your company offers to you. They aren't making it up about the high cost of health care. A simple visit to a doctor can cost over $100, and the most innocuous pills can be $80 for a teeny tiny little bottle. If something disastrous should happen, you could spend the rest of your life working just to pay off the medical bills. So most larger companies offer health insurance to their employees. Generally, the larger the company, the more generous the employers are with insurance. Unfortunately, no company is required to give you insurance. However, if they offer it to any full-time employees, they are required to offer it to all. Different companies have different waiting periods for the insurance to become effective. The waiting period can range from thirty days to a year. Walk very carefully until you are covered. You can't afford to slip up.

Sometimes the insurance premiums are completely paid for by the company, and sometimes you are asked to contribute to the costs from your paycheck. People have different needs, so some policies may cover things that others may not. You might be more interested in the health-club reimbursement offered in one plan than in the prescription drug discounts in another. Make sure you've thought about any special needs you may have before you select your coverage. In any case, unless you are made of steel and there is no kryptonite in a three-county area, you'll need health insurance. If insurance is not offered at your company, shop around for your own plan with a high deductible and affordable payments. If you can possibly afford it, it's worth it.

If insurance and other benefits are offered, someone will make you sit down and select what insurance and other benefits you want to take. Many of these plans can only be offered to you when you join the company. Because most companies only allow you to change your coverage once a year during an open-enrollment period, you'll want to know what you are doing. In order to join some plans later, you'll be required to get a doctor's statement saying you don't need the insurance. Insurance is like that. They don't want to give it to you if you actually need it.

A variety of coverages may be offered to you. Medical, dental, life, disability. The personnel department should be able to explain everything to you. But you might want to have a clue about what you want before you commit. If you don't know your indemnity from your disability, you might be stuck with choices you don't like. So, here are some simple definitions to help you through it.

MEDICAL AND DENTAL INSURANCE

HMO (Health Maintenance Organization) An HMO will usually offer you the least expensive choice for medical coverage. In order to get care, you must choose a clinic or a physician (a primary-care physician or PCP) from a list provided by the HMO. When you go to this doctor, there is a small copayment that you pay no matter what kind of treatment you get. Often the costs of prescriptions are covered or offered at a reduced cost. If you need to see a specialist, your PCP must refer you. If you are healthy and don't have a doctor you can't live without, this is the way to go. You might ask other employees to recommend doctors in the plan they like.

Many HMO plans offer special programs, like health-club reimbursements, child-ID kits, and diet group discounts. Many HMOs don't have any preexisting-condition clauses. If you are under continuous medical care, you might want to consider this, but you may not get to keep your current doctors. If you can't stand red tape, you might be frustrated in an HMO. In order to keep costs down, you have to call them to get approval to see someone practically every time you blow your nose. But if cost savings are most important to you, this is the way to go.

Indemnity Plan An indemnity plan allows you to go to any doctor or dentist you want at any time. The insurance company will pay you back a certain percentage of the costs you incur. Usually before the insurance company starts to kick in, you have to meet a certain deductible (the amount you pay out of pocket up front). Deductibles can vary a lot, so make sure you find out how much you'll be liable for if you get sick, and make sure you can afford it.

Indemnity plans tend to be more expensive, but they are more liberal about what they'll cover. Before you choose an indemnity plan, make sure they will cover any preexisting conditions that you have (any kind of continuous care you undergo, like physical rehabilitation, etc.). Every plan has limitations, so before you run out and get that nose job you've always wanted, make sure it's covered.

Employee Contribution This is the amount of money deducted from your paycheck to cover part of the cost of your insurance. Some companies will pay the whole premium for you; others ask you to chip in some of your pay. This money is usually deducted from your paycheck on a pretax basis. That means they will lower your taxable income by the amount you've paid to the plan.

Dependent Who else are you covering on your insurance? Some insurance plans only allow you to cover people the IRS recognizes as a spouse, child or elder dependent. Some, but very few, companies will allow you to cover a domestic partner.

Preexisting Condition Some policies have a clause that says that if you were already sick and knew about it when you signed up, they don't have to pay for any of the costs associated with that condition. If you are under continuous treatment for something, ask about any preexisting-condition clauses that may exist so you can try to have these costs covered too.

COBRA If you leave your company, for any reason, you are eligible to keep your current medical and dental plans for up to eighteen months. You will keep the plan at the company's rate, plus a small handling fee, but you will pay the whole premium yourself. Also, you have ninety days to decide if you want to take COBRA or not. So if you are leaving for a new job, find out how long you have to wait until your new benefits go into effect.

OTHER INSURANCE TERMS TO KNOW

Life Insurance I know you plan to live forever, but the odds are against it. If you don't have property or a family and you have no interest in being beneficent from the great beyond, you'll be OK with the minimum level of coverage offered to you. If you have property, a spouse and kids you'll need more. Be sure to take at least some life insurance, even if you don't like anyone enough to leave them a dime. Have you priced funerals lately? If you don't like them well enough to leave them anything, they surely won't spring for a decent burial for you!

Beneficiary This is who gets the money from your policies when you are gone, like in dead. This can be a family member, a friend, an institution or an organization. It's the gift that says "Ha! See how nice I was? Now don't you miss me!" (If that fiancée you listed as your beneficiary becomes your ex-fiancée, don't forget to go to personnel and change your policy.)

Long-Term Disability Unless you are made of kryptonite you probably need this. Should you become ill or injured and not be able to return to work for some time, long-term disability will pay you a percentage of your salary while you recuperate. In fact, it can keep paying until you are sixty-five if necessary. If you can't work, you don't get a salary. While your insurance covers medical expenses, how will you pay the rent, buy food or get the latest in hospital garb? If long-term disability is offered to you, take it. It's worth the peace of mind.

Accidental Death and Dismemberment (AD&D) You think you have a crummy job? There are actually people who sit in a room and figure out what a lost thumb is worth versus a lost big toe! AD&D pays a premium should you become killed or disabled in an accident. Of course being dead offers the big payoff, but I'd avoid that. However, should you become dismembered, you may want the money for tuition or to retrain for a new career. For example, if you work with computers and lose your hands, then what?

Pretax Savings Account Our friends in the IRS allow you to deduct a certain amount of money from your taxes to cover unreimbursed medical and dependent-care expenses, like your deductibles, copayments, preschool, stuff like that. A pretax savings account allows you to save this deductible money a little out of every paycheck and set up an account to save up for these things. It's sort of like funding your own little insurance plan. If you find that a medical or dental expense you know you'll need isn't covered (i.e., sessions with a therapist, glasses, or contact lenses), this is a good way to go. Make sure before you commit your money that you know what you'll spend it for. Often it's a use-it-or-lose-it proposition.

Cafeteria Plan A cafeteria plan offers you a selection of coverages at different levels and costs. For example, you might choose insurance with a high deductible (the amount you chip in before the insurance starts to pay its part) to lower your premium costs. Then you'll have money to pay for a big chunk of life insurance. It's like ordering the meat loaf so you have enough money to get the cherry jubilee. A cafeteria is a little-of-this-and-a-little-of-that kind of plan, so you can choose what you need and not pay for stuff you don't.

RETIREMENT AND PENSION PLANS

401(k) Plan A 401(k) plan lets you start saving for retirement, lower your taxable income and get in the stock market all at the same time. "Save for retirement?" you say, "I just got here!" Yes, but if you don't start socking it away now, it will be cat food and trailer parks for you when you finally leave this racket! Read all about 401(k)s in chapter 8.

Profit-Sharing/Pension Plans Some companies offer a profit-sharing plan for the benefit of their employees. This means if there is any money left over at the end of the fiscal year, they will give it to you. Most profit-sharing plans are vested. That means, if you leave in a couple of years, they might take the money back; but the longer you work there, the more you get to keep when you leave or retire. For example, if you leave a company in two years, they may have put some money in a plan for you, but you won't get to take it. However, if you've worked there four years, they might let you have 30 percent of the money when you leave (you are 30 percent vested); and at ten years, you can have it all (you are 100 percent vested). This money is meant for retirement, and there are substantial penalties and taxes involved if you take the money out early and don't roll it over into a new plan.

Rollover Rolling over means taking the money you have saved in your profit-sharing and 401(k) plans and rolling it directly into another tax-deferred vehicle, like an IRA. If you've been able to save money without paying taxes on it, the IRS will give you a penalty if you use the money before you retire. You'll want to avoid touching all that lovely money and put it right into another tax-deferred account.

OTHER BENEFITS

Tuition Reimbursement I know you just escaped from the Ivory Tower, but you might find that certain courses can help you do a better job and make you more valuable (translate into salary increases). Many companies have a tuition-reimbursement plan. Check it out with the personnel manager or in the employee handbook. The courses that will be reimbursed usually must have something to do with your profession. If your manager asks you to take a course, see if the company will pay for it in full.

Sick Days Some companies will pay you to be sick, which is certainly something no one else will do for you. If you get the flu and can't come to work, they will pay you anyway. The number of days varies from company to company. Once you have exceeded those days, they will start to take

away your vacation. Before you play hooky for weeks at a
time, remember that you can be terminated if you take too
many sick days. If you are really unable to work for more
than one week, then you should talk to your employer
about going on medical leave and using the disability plans.

Vacation Days Most companies allow for a certain number
of paid vacation days. Hallelujah! Again this varies from
company to company and how long you've been with the
place. Some places won't let you take any vacation until
you've been there for six months; so if you've got to be in
a wedding in Peru for a week, let someone know sooner
rather than later. Another trick about vacation days is that
you can lose them if you don't take them. That is, if you
don't take your two weeks this year, you won't have four
weeks saved up for next year. If your work load makes it
impossible for you to take your vacation when you need
to, ask your supervisor for a note saying you can hold your
time until the following year. Verbal promises are often
forgotten even in the unlikelihood that you are still working
for the same person a year from now. You keep a copy
and ask personnel to keep a copy in your file.

Maternity/Medical Leave Most companies make provisions
for maternity leave. You may or may not be paid for some
or all of your time away from work. The law requires that
your job, or a comparable job, be kept available to you for
up to twelve weeks should you or someone in your family
have a medical emergency. This is called the Family Medical
Leave Act. It's relatively new, so some companies won't
know to offer it to you should you need to take care of a
sick relative or require a medical leave yourself. Your com-

pany is not required to pay you, only to keep your job for you. For more information on maternity/medical leave, see the Legalities section, which follows.

LEGALITIES

Employment laws vary from state to state. Contact the Department of Labor if you need further details. Here are some guidelines you should know about.

Overtime Overtime eligibility is based on job duties, not on titles. So they can call you Senior Vice President of Mail Room Clerks, but you still are entitled to overtime pay. Generally, in the broadest possible strokes, eligibility for overtime pay is based on how independently you work, how many decisions you are asked to make on your own, and if you manage or supervise other people. If you are eligible for overtime, it is based on a forty-hour work week. That means that you must work forty hours in a week before the overtime at time-and-a-half kicks in. (PHRASE TO THROW AROUND: "My sister works for the Department of Labor and she says . . .")

Paydays Most companies pay either weekly or on the fifteenth and last days of the month. It is illegal to hold up your paycheck for any reason if you are a full-time employee. They can't hold back your paycheck until you turn in an expense report, or complete a task or for any other reason. If you are not paid on time, you can raise a stink about it. (PHRASE TO THROW AROUND: Treble Damages.)

Worker's Compensation If you are injured during work or performing a job duty even out of the office itself, you are entitled to Worker's Compensation. This will pay any medical bills associated with this injury. You can even claim it if you get sick from the bad shrimp at the company Christmas party (just be sure it's not a hangover), if you cut your finger working on something and need stitches or get in a car accident running a company errand. If the company is really psycho, you can even try to claim shrink bills!

Employment Contracts Most companies do not offer contracts for entry-level jobs in the United States, although this is a common practice overseas. If you are offered a contract, make sure it spells out terms such as severance pay, notice (yours and theirs), job title, and start date. Also ask to see the employee handbook, so that these contract conditions are not less than stated in their regular policy.

Time Off Companies have different policies about vacation. Paid time off is a benefit that, if offered, you should try to take advantage of. It's good for you! Find out from the personnel manager if it is a use-it-or-lose-it proposition (that is, it doesn't carry over from year to year) or if it keeps adding up if you don't take it. If you work in a use-it-or-lose-it company and a heavy workload keeps you from taking your scheduled vacation, ask your supervisor to give you a note that says she agrees that you can take the vacation late. Give a copy of it to personnel, and keep a copy. Also, find out how many sick days you are entitled to in a year. If you exceed this amount, it can result in excess absenteeism and can be grounds to terminate you. PHRASE TO MUTTER AS YOU WALK PAST PERSONNEL: "If I don't get a break soon, we are talking Worker's Compensation."

Unemployment If you are a permanent full-time or even a full-time/temporary employee, you are probably entitled to unemployment benefits if you are laid off or fired. You are not entitled to unemployment benefits if you resign (so think twice about that righteous indignation) or if you are fired for cause. Cause is defined as the willful disregard of company rules (i.e., you wear your pajamas every day to a place where there is a strict dress code), you steal, you are habitually late or absent, you slug somebody or refuse to perform an assigned duty. If you are terminated for poor performance, you are entitled to benefits. You can find the location of your nearest unemployment office in the yellow pages. Be sure to call first so you can bring along any documentation they require. PHRASE TO THROW AROUND IN THE UNEMPLOYMENT LINE: "Excuse me, I am supposed to pick up my Thorazine in a half an hour. Do you think we'll be done by then?"

Maternity/Family Medical Leave Act (FMLA) Companies have varying policies about how or if they pay you during a maternity or medical leave. However, the federal law requires that your position, or a comparable one stay open and available to you for ninety days. In order to avoid sexual discrimination in the plan, all medical leaves for maternity or for any type of surgery should be covered at the same pay rate. It is at the company's discretion if you will be paid full, partial or any salary during that time. You are eligible to continue your insurance during your leave. Your physician determines how long you can be out.

Make sure you notify personnel after your baby is born so it can be added to your medical policy and be covered too. Short-term disability should pay you during the recovery time for a pregnancy, usually six weeks for a regular delivery and ten weeks for a C-section.

Americans with Disabilities Act (ADA) Federal law requires that companies make a reasonable accommodation to make a work site fully accessible to employees with disabilities. This includes desks high enough for wheelchair access, amplified phones and other adjustments to the space and equipment that might be necessary. You cannot be turned down for a job or a promotion because of any physical disabilities. The company is required to accommodate your needs.

Benefit Eligibility In order to receive benefits on a pretax basis, companies have eligibility requirements. All employees who are scheduled to work a certain number of hours a week (usually a minimum of twenty-five) are entitled to benefits. However, all employees in the company must have the same eligibility. There may be a waiting period after your hire date before you are eligible to join the plans. Also all employees no matter how many hours worked in a week are entitled to social security, unemployment and worker's compensation. PHRASE TO MAKE THEM THINK THEY CAN'T PUT ANYTHING OVER ON YOU: "If I'm not eligible for benefits, won't that throw you out of compliance?"

COBRA If you have received health insurance through your company, you are always eligible to continue to stay on the plan *at your own expense* for up to eighteen months. This is true whether you quit or are terminated. You also have ninety days to decide if you want to take continued benefits or not; you are not required to decide on your last day on the job. WORDS TO SHOW THEM YOU ARE SMARTER THAN THEY THINK YOU ARE: "Consolidated Omnibus Budget Reconciliation Act. Heard of it?"

Severance Pay If you are terminated for "cause" (see the section on unemployment), a company is not required to pay you severance. In fact, in most states companies are not required to pay severance at all. Still, most companies pay a week's severance in lieu of notice. But again, make sure you read the company handbook for the policy. If it is not published there, you should ask to see the policy; they are required to show it to you. If they don't have a written policy, oh happy day. Trust me, all you have to do is ask to see the policy, and you'll be getting a severance check!

Notice, Yours When you leave a job, it is considered good form to give two weeks' notice. This gives the company time to find a replacement for you and to wrap up what you've started. Often they would like you to start your new job right away, but they should understand that you don't want to burn bridges where you are. So unless there is an extraordinary reason not to, give two weeks. Your last check should include pay to your final day and any unused vacation time. You don't get severance pay when you resign. Sometimes if you go to work for a competitor, your current employer will ask you to leave right away. If they do, they should pay you for the "notice" period, even if you aren't in the office.

Notice, Theirs On the other hand, many states do not require that you be given any notice if you are to lose your
job. For performance-based issues, this varies from state to
state. So yes, they can fire you and not pay you past your
last day in the office. You may be paid out "notice in lieu
of severance." That means they will pay you the two weeks'
notice they should have given you, if you'll only go home
right now. If you are concerned, contact the local department of labor and ask what your rights are. WORDS TO
MAKE THEM SCRAMBLE: "According to the policy . . ."
Or if there is no policy: "I know that Mary got . . ."

Harassment Racial, age, religious or sexual harassment of
any sort is against the law. If you believe you are being
harassed, bring it to the attention of personnel immediately.
The company is required to discuss with you what you
would like to do about it (it doesn't mean they have to do
it if you want them to, but they must take some action on
your behalf). Then they must take steps to make sure the
harassment stops. Management cannot transfer you to a
different or lesser position against your wishes in order to
get you away from the harasser. If someone needs to be
transferred, it's the harasser. If the harassment continues,
see personnel again. At this point, if the problem persists,
and nothing more is done, see an attorney.